AF600247

A RESEARCH AGENDA FOR GRADUATE EDUCATION

A Research Agenda for Graduate Education

BRIAN S. MITCHELL

UNIVERSITY OF TORONTO PRESS
Toronto Buffalo London

Toronto Buffalo London
utorontopress.com

ISBN 978-1-4875-0861-6 (cloth) ISBN 978-1-4875-3862-0 (EPUB)
ISBN 978-1-4875-3861-3 (PDF)

Library and Archives Canada Cataloguing in Publication

Title: A research agenda for graduate education / Brian S. Mitchell.
Names: Mitchell, Brian S., 1962– author.
Description: Includes bibliographical references and index.
Identifiers: Canadiana (print) 20210158352 | Canadiana (ebook) 20210158468 | ISBN 9781487508616 (cloth) | ISBN 9781487538613 (PDF) | ISBN 9781487538620 (EPUB)
Subjects: LCSH: Education, Higher – Research. | LCSH: Universities and colleges – Graduate work.
Classification: LCC LB2326.3 .M58 2021 | DDC 378.0072 – dc23

University of Toronto Press acknowledges the financial assistance to its publishing program of the Canada Council for the Arts and the Ontario Arts Council, an agency of the Government of Ontario.

Canada Council for the Arts
Conseil des Arts du Canada

Funded by the Government of Canada
Financé par le gouvernement du Canada

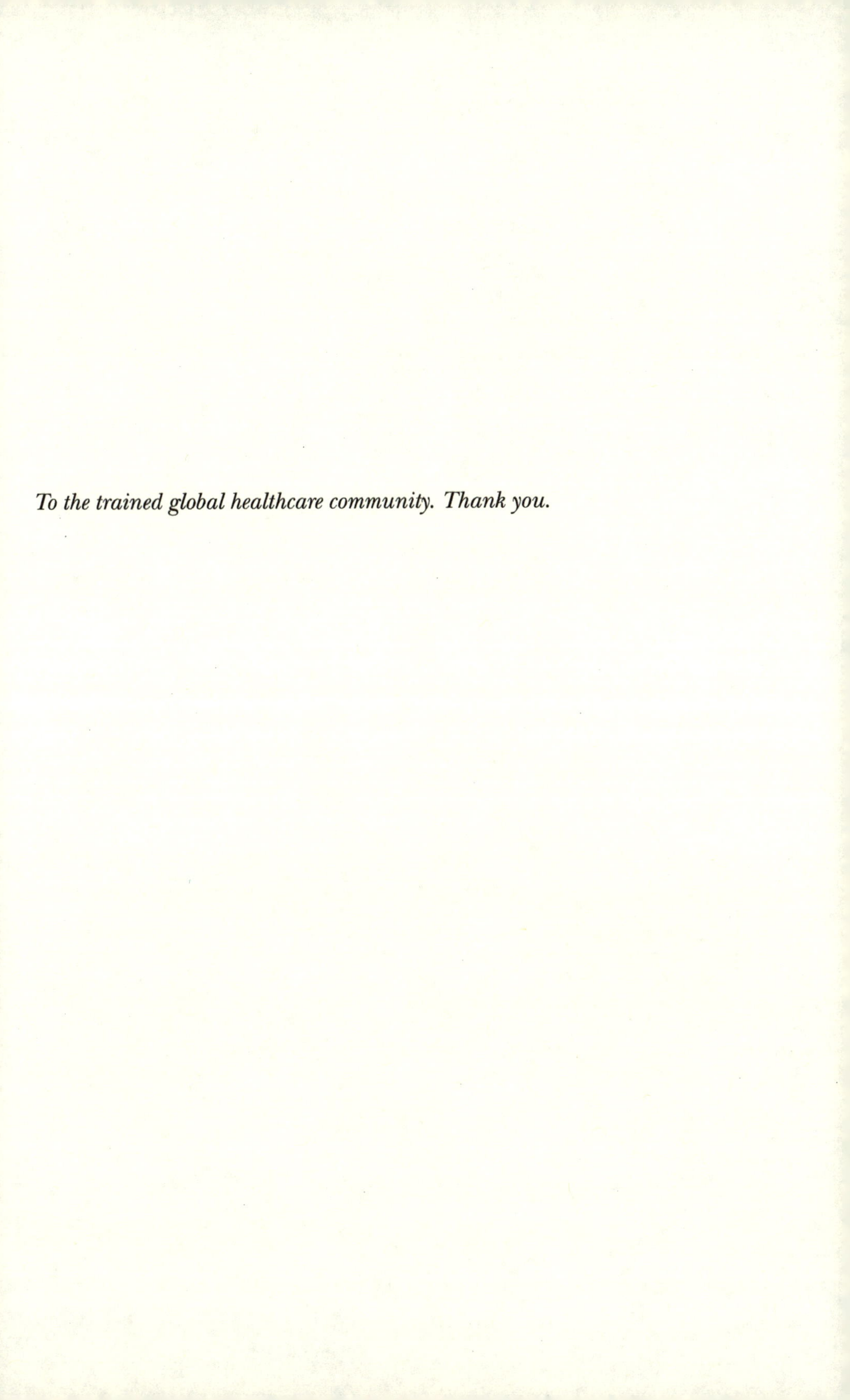

To the trained global healthcare community. Thank you.

Contents

Figures and Tables

Figures

Tables

Foreword

As I write, it is late fall 2020 – a time of devastating global pandemic, climate change, rising nationalism, and vividly exposed long-standing racial and economic fault lines. Two things are clear: we have never needed graduate-prepared scientists and scholars, citizens, and leaders more; and universities and funding agencies have never needed more to sharply focus investments on the graduate programs and pedagogies that these thinkers and doers must have.

The need for better data on graduate program learning outcomes, for the alignment of those outcomes with changing workforce demands, and for funding models that best encourage access to and completion of high-quality graduate education is not new. Today's troubles simply make that need more urgent. So, Brian Mitchell's monograph could not have come at a better time. In it, he outlines a comprehensive framework and set of research questions that would provide the data necessary to enhance graduate student learning and career preparation and improve graduate programs.

Take, for example, chapter 1 on the science of graduate-level learning. As Dr. Mitchell notes, graduate online learning has been taking place for at least two decades. Full online degree programs have been predominantly at the master's level but an increasing number of doctoral programs are making that transition. Thus, he asks, "Can the development of research methods in the PhD be transitioned to self-paced and/or electronic delivery?" He then goes on to explore the intersection between acquisition of research and teaching skills and challenges researchers to devise studies to address questions such as "Which specific research skills do teaching experiences impact most?" and "Do research skills impact teaching effectiveness?" Later in this same chapter, in particularly insightful, and near prescient, sections on mentoring and learning in online environments, the author engages questions regarding learning outcomes in distance-delivered graduate programs and approaches to understanding what constitutes effective e-mentoring.

Consider now the extremely rapid, pandemic-induced transition from in-person to nearly ubiquitous online graduate learning in March 2020. Universities around the world rapidly pivoted to online didactic learning and began experimenting with creating virtual research teams and projects. Throughout the summer and fall of 2020, presentations at numerous higher education association meetings began to share ongoing experiments with virtual peer and faculty mentorship. Clearly the higher education enterprise has demonstrated agility and a deep commitment to its students. Yet, as argued in this monograph, without a rigorous research and evaluation framework to measure the efficacy of the models being piloted, these noble experiments will remain just that, leaving us to wonder which of the models actually work, which are dead ends, and what investments we could make that might improve any or all of them.

None of us have a crystal ball but of one thing we can be certain: the future of work will not be a simple linear extrapolation of its past. Current graduate students will enter first jobs that may not have existed at the time they started their graduate programs. They will change jobs and employment sectors more often than in the past and the route they take throughout those careers will look more like a London tube map than an interstate highway. How will graduate programs and faculty help to prepare their students for this changing work environment? As the comprehensive literature review included in this monograph demonstrates, it is far from glib to say more research is needed. In chapter 2 on graduate student career preparation, the author lays out a research agenda that could inform curricular redesign and inform design and implementation of the professional development opportunities necessary to help students prepare for evolving careers. In a powerful concluding section to this chapter, Dr. Mitchell asks us to consider how we might reimagine and measure the very nature of what is considered career success.

In a final chapter, made all the more pressing given the serious financial pressures that universities around the globe are experiencing, the author calls for research that will help universities marshal financial-aid packages in ways that maximize opportunities for both access and timely degree completion. He challenges researchers and the graduate education community writ large to move beyond a singular focus on representational diversity at the point of admission to a broader understanding of the undergraduate-to-graduate pathway and the climates of inclusiveness necessary for graduate student well-being – points rendered even more urgent by current events.

I have had the privilege of working directly with Brian during the years he served as the Council of Graduate Schools/National Science Foundation (CGS/NSF) Dean-in-Residence. During his time with us, I learned a great deal from him, as did CGS staff and community. This monograph is rooted in his deep understanding of the graduate ecosystem and the kinds of research needed to make it even more responsive to changing student demographics and changing social and economic contexts. I am absolutely delighted that his wisdom and insights will now be shared with an even broader community.

Suzanne Ortega
President, Council of Graduate Schools

Preface

Why does the graduate education community need a research agenda? For the same reason that course instructors have syllabi, that federal agencies require proposals upon which to base awards, that companies and institutions conduct annual personnel evaluations and tenure reviews, and that automobiles have GPS: so that we know where we've been, where we're going, and how to get there. And just like in all of those examples, there are multiple ways to get there. This is just one outline for how to generate more data and better models related to graduate education that not only build on existing research but forge new areas of inquiry. University administrators want up-to-date and robust data upon which to base decisions. Employers want to know that their future employees will have requisite skills. Faculty want to know that their curricula and mentoring practices are relevant and subject to continuous improvement. Graduate students want value for their education and prospective students want information with which to make informed career choices. I argue that the key purveyors of graduate education – graduate faculty and graduate school administrators – do not have the same deep understanding of research on graduate education that they have (or had) for their own disciplinary scholarship. I see no difference in the approach that should be taken. There is much to know and there are many problems to be solved. A sound, scholarly approach will invariably generate meaningful results.

What Do We Know about Graduate Education?

Despite the ominous opening, it turns out that a fair amount of information is available on graduate education, at least from a historical perspective. *The Formation of Scholars* (Walker et al., 2008) provides a data-driven historical view of graduate education in the United States as well as key talking points around which to re-envision graduate education. The historical importance of graduate education to the North American higher education landscape is reflected in the history of the Association of Graduate Schools (AGS), where the PhD as a key driver in the formation of the Association of American Universities (AAU) is described (Slate, 1994). A good follow-up to these two books is *Reforming Doctoral Education, 1990 to 2015* (Weisbuch & Cassuto, 2016). Annual reports from the National Science Foundation's National Center for Science and Engineering (National Center for Science and Engineering Statistics, 2019a) and US Department of Education (Kena et al., 2016), as well as periodic reports from international organizations such as the Organisation for Economic Co-operation and Development (Auriol et al., 2013) provide timely data for the graduate education community to analyze. Seminal works in the peer-reviewed literature provide keen insight into such topics as mentoring, financial aid, persistence and retention in graduate school, and diversity at all stages of education and in the workforce. *ASHE Higher Education Reports* have been a key contributor as well, such as the 2001 monograph on socialization of graduate and professional students (Weidman et al., 2001) and the 2009 monograph on the development of doctoral students (Gardner, 2009). An implicit theme runs through the past century of graduate education literature: despite its flaws, graduate education is important. Otherwise, why continue to talk and write about it? It may not work quite how everyone wants it to all the time, but there are enough salary and employment metrics both in the United States (Kena et al., 2016) and abroad (Diamond et al., 2014), and historical indicators such as enrollment and attainment growth rate (Okahana et al., 2016) to suggest that some things are done correctly. But sufficiently detailed evidence is lacking as to how or why graduate education works, so when policy crises arise there are little hard data and few reliable models upon which to rely.

How Is Graduate Education Changing?

Moreover, things change – sometimes rapidly. Problem areas of graduate education range from the chronic, such as the lack of diversity in both student and faculty populations (Mayhew, 1972; Mayhew, 1980), to the cumulative, such as an overemphasis on professoriate careers in the humanities (Cassuto, 2015). These concerns have led to a common narrative in the graduate education community that graduate students should be prepared for multiple careers, especially careers outside the academy. Efforts to implement change have come from data-driven recommendations, as in the biomedical sciences where the US National Institutes of Health

(NIH) commissioned a report on the biomedical workforce (National Institutes of Health, 2012) and followed up on a key recommendation by creating the Broadening Experiences in Scientific Training (BEST) Program. Professional societies increasingly have been introspective in the career preparation of their graduate students (ACS, 2013; American Academy of Arts and Sciences, 2015; Czujko & Anderson, 2015; Fiske et al., 2010; Grafton & Grossman, 2011). Non-governmental organizations such as the Council of Graduate Schools (Allum et al., 2014; Wendler et al., 2010; Wendler et al., 2012), Pew Charitable Trusts (Golde & Dore, 2001), and the National Academies of Sciences, Engineering and Medicine (National Academies of Sciences, Engineering, and Medicine, 2018; National Research Council, 2005) have been key drivers in changing the conversations surrounding graduate student career preparation and federal higher education policy implementation. Despite these efforts, graduate education has changed little during the past century. What has certainly changed is the environment in which it finds itself, including funding structures, the growth of professional development activities, and an increased emphasis on interdisciplinary scholarship. All these changes have implications for the way graduate students are trained.

What Types of Research Does Graduate Education Most Need?

Reports, reviews, and historical summaries of graduate education and its defining metrics are important; however, they are limiting in that they are primarily retrospective and not longitudinal. As a result, they tend not to be predictive. For example, the most recent quasi-decanal assessment of doctoral programs from the US National Research Council (Ostriker et al., 2011) relies upon data collected from a single academic year (2005–6). Although such reports certainly have utility, they do not reflect the current state of these programs, nor do they describe the processes by which they achieved the status reflected in the report. What is missing from graduate education research is more timely data, longitudinal studies across a wider array of institution types, and theoretically sound and robust models on more specific research questions that consider multiple factors and their interactions. This research could be both qualitative and quantitative and could employ mixed methods, but its results should be as generalizable as possible across time and disciplines.

A key example is in the areas of diversity and inclusion. An entire section is dedicated to diversity and inclusion later in this monograph and these topics permeate virtually all the research questions that are posed in the other sections, but a brief introduction here serves to illustrate the point. A recent research article (Gibbs et al., 2016) comes from the world of the biomedical sciences, which is currently one of the most well-researched disciplines in the graduate education literature. The simulations of Gibbs et al. predict that faculty diversity will not increase significantly in the next four decades through increases in the underrepresented minority (URM) graduate school population or open faculty positions alone, but through increased rates of transitions from postdoctoral candidates into the academy. This result may seem intuitive; however, it provides evidence from which extrapolations can be made. This type of research on graduate education is compelling for several reasons. First, it addresses a timely and important issue in graduate education, namely diversity. Second, it not only utilizes data over a long period (1980–2014) but correlates individuals across data sets, in this case from completion of the PhD to attainment of an assistant professor position. Third, it employs sound statistical methods and uses simulations to run "what-if" scenarios that would otherwise be impractical, impossible, or unethical to perform in real life.

Not all research on graduate education need be this quantitative, nor must diversity-related research be limited to racial and ethnic diversity. A mixed-methods study (Feldon et al., 2016) on skills development in STEM students found that skill inequality differs from other forms of inequality such as socioeconomic status or gender, with implications on how to address it prior to enrollment in graduate school. What is interesting about this study is that it represents not only a mixed-methods approach but a collaboration of investigators from four different institutions and scholarly backgrounds. Their work, however, is based upon existing socialization theory models that will be described in chapter 2.

There are numerous additional examples to come in the ensuing pages from various disciplines and countries on a variety of graduate education topics. Regardless of discipline, these examples generally meet the following criteria: they are published in the peer-reviewed, indexed literature (discoverable using Web of Science, SCOPUS, PubMed, or Google Scholar); they address a specific issue in graduate education that is well-defined and timely; they reflect a unique combination of investigator expertise; they employ sound research methods, whether qualitative, quantitative, or mixed; and they provide hard evidence that allows (at least in theory) faculty and administrators to propose and implement change.

These foundational studies and others like them are organized into three general categories: the science of learning at the graduate level, preparation for a career with an advanced degree, and graduate program improvement. I selected these three areas because I see them representing the target audiences. Those who study graduate education –

educational psychologists working on theories and mechanisms of teaching and learning at the graduate level, for example – will be most interested in the first chapter. Those who are deeply involved in delivering graduate education – primarily research faculty – will be most interested in the second chapter. They are the ones who can provide evidence on how student-centered programs are working. Chapter 3 will be of most interest to administrators and policy makers involved in graduate education. They are the agents of change at the program and institutional levels. Certainly there are other ways to organize the research topics, such as a disciplinary-based approach, but this monograph advocates against such siloed thinking. Similarly, organization by theories of learning presupposes that all theories are currently known and undermines the underlying premise that new theories are needed. In the current educational research landscape so little is being done on graduate education that broad appeal is necessary, even if that means only one chapter might be relevant to a particular group.

Finally, this research agenda is not just an updated literature review or organization of existing research on graduate education. The monograph should offer those things at least, but at most it aspires to identify gaps in the literature, enumerate the limitations of the research that in most cases have already been identified by the authors themselves, coalesce the needs and shortcomings in graduate education research around common themes, and give some guidance on how that research might be best carried out and disseminated.

Acknowledgments

The author wishes to thank the reviewers and numerous colleagues from the graduate education community at the Council of Graduate Schools and the Division of Graduate Education at the National Science Foundation who provided critical input to the development of this monograph. Any opinions, findings, conclusions, or recommendations expressed herein are those of the author and do not necessarily reflect the views of the Council of Graduate Schools or the National Science Foundation. The support of the Carol Lavin Bernick Faculty Grant Program is gratefully acknowledged.

A RESEARCH AGENDA FOR GRADUATE EDUCATION

Introduction

A profound incongruence exists in graduate education. The very foundation upon which advanced degrees is built – research – is critically neglected when it comes to graduate student learning, career preparation, and program improvement. This lack of scholarly investigation and introspection is due, in part, to the fact that the graduate education community is highly heterogeneous. It comprises faculty mentors, higher education administrators, educational researchers, students, and investors (policy makers, funding agencies, and governing boards) who share the common goal of training scholars of the highest level so that they will contribute to the intellectual and economic growth of nations and the world but who lack a unified vision when it comes to charting a course for advancing their common goals. The faculty who deliver graduate education are by and large exceptional scholars within their respective disciplines but have little understanding beyond the anecdotal of how or why, historically, an apprenticeship-based model works. Graduate deans, school deans, and other university administrators deeply value graduate education but have a paucity of comparative information at their disposal with which to make difficult programmatic and budgetary decisions. Researchers on higher education have prodigious social-science and educational-psychology tools at their disposal but may lack access to (and buy-in from) the disciplinary faculty that are the gatekeepers of graduate degree programs. The investors promote and provide the lifeblood of financial support for graduate education in selected fields, requiring proof of efficacy and return on investment as accountability. Students simply want information with which to make important life choices. These constituencies would benefit from responsible and robust research on graduate education; however, such research is lacking.

The importance of interdisciplinary investigation on graduate education transcends these pragmatic considerations. Ultimately, graduate education opportunities exist for the benefit of the students and their careers. Without these emerging scholars, considerably less new knowledge is generated and the next generation of trained innovators is lost. Any attempts at moving the graduate education community forward should then focus on understanding and improving graduate student training. Such guided inquiry provides three general types of substantive benefit. First, the science of the graduate-level learning spectrum is expanded. Much appropriate attention is paid to pedagogy, educational psychology, and outcomes assessment at the pre-K and undergraduate (P–16) levels. How does learning change for those who undertake graduate-level training and are more advanced in their cognitive development? Second, workforces are evolving, not just in terms of demographics but in terms of requisite skills and career ecosystems. How should the career preparation of graduate students anticipate the malleable professions that await them? Finally, more and better research provides information, evidence, models, and guidance for graduate degree program improvement. Well beyond the descriptive statistics of time to degree, numbers of publications, or persistence rates, how are new and effective activities incorporated into both old and new programs and how are those that are antiquated and ineffective jettisoned? Indeed, how does one even know what practices are effective and which never were?

A plan would help guide this inquiry. That plan should be based upon the current state of knowledge. It should be rooted in rigorous research methodologies that move beyond descriptive statistics of historical data and into the realm of simulation and modeling. Such a plan would allow us to test long-standing educational theories and obtain information on groups of students that are too small to sample with statistical significance. It should seek to explore new areas of graduate training that did not exist 10, 20, or 40 years ago, as well as answer long-lingering questions. For example, the debate over the optimal method of graduate student funding has been raging for decades. Fifty years ago there was a "crisis" in graduate education with the proposed redirection of federal support for graduate-student traineeships to individual research projects (Are graduate students worth keeping? 1970). Today the converse conversation is taking place (Blume-Kohout & Adhikari, 2016; National Science and Technology Council, 2013; Pickett et al., 2015). Comprehensive reviews and expert reports provide meaningful historical snapshots of the state of graduate education (Berelson, 1960a). Opinion pieces on the meaning of graduate training help shape thought processes (Cuthbert & Molla, 2015; McCook, 2011; Taylor, 2011); however, there are few quantitative, qualitative, and mixed-methods studies that rigorously test existing models or propose and test new ones. In an effort to provide a structured framework to help identify topics and encourage collaborative research teams, a series of overarching research questions is proposed here, grouped into the three areas of benefit outlined above. The working principle is a simple one: there is as much (or more) to know and learn about graduate education as there is at any other level of teaching and learning.

Terminology and Degree Categories

Nowhere are disciplinary differences more evident than in conversations on graduate education. Even the term "graduate education" requires contextualization. In most settings outside of North America, it is termed "post-graduate education." In this monograph it means the curricular and co-curricular activities related to students enrolled in post-baccalaureate degree programs. This definition is meant to provide reasonable bounds to the research questions but not to be exclusionary where relevance may otherwise dictate. For example, studies of graduate-level online learning environments may be useful to those studying continuing education or post-graduate certifications via virtual learning environments. The focus of online learning here, however, will be on graduate degree–seeking students. Similarly, some of the research questions might explore pre–graduate school factors that affect post–graduate school career success. The link here will always be through the graduate school experience.

Other terminology requiring clarification comes directly from the degree programs. The term "graduate degree" will be used as frequently and generically as possible to refer to any post-baccalaureate degree. The terms "doctoral" and "master's" will be used to refer to degrees and degree programs defined by most US accrediting bodies (48 and 30 credit hours or equivalent, respectively) when that distinction is necessary; terms such as "professional" and "non-professional" to describe degrees and degree programs will be used only sparingly as they tend to convolute rather than clarify program distinctions. To be clear, much of the focus here is on the PhD degree and less on degrees such as the JD, MD, or MSW. This is not a statement of importance. We will see in the next section that there is robust literature in key areas of graduate training such as the health sciences (especially nursing), much of which is driven by professional society accreditation needs and by disciplinary culture. As a result, many of the identified gaps in the literature are related to the other degrees, such as the research doctorate. Finally, the term "research degree" will be used to specify the subset of graduate degrees and programs that have a clear research product as the culminating experience, namely a thesis, dissertation, or the equivalent. Specific research questions about research degrees may be relevant to all advanced degrees; the term "non-research" will not be used to describe graduate students, degrees, or programs as it is unnecessarily exclusionary.

With respect to students and their careers, much care is required not only to clarify terminology for the purposes of this monograph but also to attempt to change the manner in which these subjects are discussed. For example, the terms "academic" and "non-academic" when used to describe the careers of those with graduate degrees have at the very least led to confusion on the purpose of a graduate degree for would-be students and employers and at worst been damaging to the graduate-education community writ large. "Academic careers" may be a totally accurate descriptor for the subset of graduate degree holders who enter the professoriate but, when used as a comparator with those who do not, it establishes a false dichotomy. As one of my graduate dean colleagues (an excellent scholar of comparative literature in his own right) once pointed out to me, when using terms like "hard" and "soft" (as when describing professional skills), "hard" always wins. In this monograph, such binary descriptors are replaced with a more nuanced but continuum-based view of graduate education. Terms like "compatible careers" or "multiple careers" may be less descriptive but are more inclusive. It is in this spirit that some terms heretofore ensconced in the graduate education lexicon are purposely eschewed.

When it comes to describing individual degrees and degree requirements, some structure is needed. Nobody likes being put in a box; however, organizational structure and individuality are not mutually exclusive concepts. There is utility in structure insofar as it prompts us to ask important questions about graduate education programs. Should a thesis or dissertation be required for this degree and, if so, for what purpose? How much coursework is necessary for the development of a working professional and/or independent scholar in the field? Structure can provide the starting point for these important conversations – not just for the development of new degree programs but for the formative and summative evaluation of existing ones. That organizational structure most commonly comes in the form of degree types. There is little disagreement on the first level of distinction by degree type: master's and doctorate. This bifurcation is important to employers, accrediting bodies, professional societies, universities that must continuously hire faculty at the necessary level of credentialing, and the faculty who must develop and deliver the graduate-level curricula. The second level of differentiation is where disagreement sets in. Degrees at the master's and doctoral levels traditionally have been labeled as belonging to either the "research" or "professional" genre. The dual MD-PhD degrees in the biomedical sciences, for example, are a clear indication that this differentiation is important. In other disciplines, however, the PhD is considered the "professional" degree insofar as it endows students with the only degree appropriate for a professional career in that area. At the master's level, there is even more confusion. For example, the establishment of and recent reinvigorated interest in the Professional Science Master's (PSM) and Professional Master of Arts (PMA) degrees have attempted to draw clear curricular boundaries between research and professional master's programs. Fortunately, this research/professional distinction has limited use at the master's level for the purposes of this monograph. The focus will be on sound research methodologies. If there is an interesting study from the world of graduate-level nursing education that has broad relevance, for example, then it will be described here. Conversely, the data-collection methods used for studying the mobility of doctoral researchers, for example, may have implications for those working on a similar topic in related degree fields such as law and dentistry.

The focus here will be on the end product: good research on graduate education performed by qualified research teams that employ sound research practices. How should these research products be disseminated? Ideally, they should be available in peer-reviewed literature. Unlike books and monographs that must be either purchased by individuals or libraries and are (generally) available only to one user at a time, journal publications are freely accessible (but certainly not free) to multiple researchers at a time. The information in journal articles is generally more timely and more narrowly focused on specific research results. If published in the right places, journal-based research results are rigorously peer reviewed. Books may also be reviewed; however, the depth of review tends to be less pronounced due simply to limited time and limited availability of the primary information. Finally, research in journal articles is more readily accessed through citation indexes. How researchers search for journal articles may be changing but access is still gained using university licenses. With the rise of open-access research publications this, too, may be changing. The broad availability of journal articles exposes graduate-education research to a more scholastically diverse audience and fosters cross-disciplinary conversations on graduate education. This is not to say that all research on graduate education should be disseminated through journal articles. The graduate-education community needs books and monographs to bring broad perspectives on important topics. It needs opinions. It needs commissioned reports from experts in the field. Foundational research on graduate education is also necessary. Such primary works are best disseminated in indexed literature for all to access and cite.

The Literature

The literature devoted to graduate education is broad, if not altogether deep, and falls into the three general categories named above: books and monographs, reports, and peer-reviewed journal articles. Since the bulk of this monograph is dedicated to analyzing graduate education research disseminated in citable journal articles, an exhaustive review of the numerous books and monographs on this subject will not be given here. Similarly, there is a substantial number of reports on graduate education from federal agencies, professional societies, and educational centers but they quickly become dated and are not always easily found in the indexed literature or through online searches. Nevertheless, books and reports serve a useful purpose to the graduate education community, especially with respect to summarizing the peer-reviewed literature of the time, so a brief overview of the contributions from these two broad sources is in order.

Graduate Education in the United States (Berelson, 1960b), first published in 1960, is a well-referenced history of graduate education in the United States from its inception through the middle of the 20th century. It is relevant to note that even historical texts such as this contain a high level of editorial content, as illustrated by the following excerpt:

> It is clear that the mere presence of criticism is not enough to warrant serious change. Criticism is endemic in the educational world and will be as long as clear measures of the quality of the product are not available. (Berelson, 1960b)

Other books followed, focusing on the research component of graduate education worldwide (Clark, 1993), updates to previous books (Nerad et al., 1997), specific historical periods (Blume & Amsterdamska, 1987; Mayhew, 1980; Slate, 1994), the doctorate (Blessinger & Stockley, 2016; Bowen & Rudenstine, 1992; Noble, 1994), and most recently doctoral education in the humanities (Cassuto, 2015). *The Formation of Scholars* is the 21st-century equivalent of *Graduate Education in the United States* in the sense that it presents research findings in a historical context and makes recommendations and observations that are eerily reminiscent of those made a half-century earlier: "Although education at other levels is being reshaped by new knowledge about how people learn, these same insights seem to have washed over graduate education with little effect" (Walker et al., 2008, p. 4).

Reports convey similar opinions and findings. Limiting the discussion to reports from the past 20 years or so and leaving the review of previous reports to the history books, the call for reform in graduate education has been clear and focused on career preparation. *The Path Forward* (Wendler et al., 2010) and related follow-on reports (Allum et al., 2014; Okahana, 2019; Okahana & Kinoshita, 2018; Wendler et al., 2012) from the Council of Graduate Schools (CGS) and its partners as well as reports from professional societies such as the American Anthropological Association (Fiske et al., 2010), American Chemical Society (ACS, 2013), American Institute of Physics (Czujko & Anderson, 2015), the US National Academies (Committee on Science, Engineering, and Public Policy, 1995; National Academies of Sciences, Engineering, and Medicine, 2018; National Research Council, 2005) and Organisation for Economic Co-operation and Development (OECD) (Auriol et al., 2012; Auriol et al., 2013) have all promoted preparing graduate students for multiple careers. Other reports focus on the periodic dissemination of important metrics in graduate education (National Center for Science and Engineering Statistics, 2017b; Okahana et al., 2016), international collaborations and developments (Appelt et al., 2015), the economic impact of graduate education (Diamond et al., 2014), and historical trends (National Center for Science and Engineering Statistics, 2019a). But little foundational research is reported through such reports; even if it is, it may not be peer reviewed.

The focus of this monograph is on foundational research in graduate education as reported in peer-reviewed literature. A Web of Science (WoS) search for articles on both graduate and undergraduate education shows that the absolute number of articles on graduate education has generally grown exponentially since 2000 (figure 1a).[1] A search using the term "postgraduate education" as used outside of North America is provided for comparison (more on this distinction in a moment). The ratio of undergraduate-level articles to graduate education–related articles has shown modest but inconsistent growth over the past two decades, with roughly 20% more undergraduate than graduate education articles. Given the substantially larger enrollments in baccalaureate programs over graduate programs in North America, research on graduate education would appear to be in fine standing. Similarly, doctoral education publications outnumber master's-level education publications (figure 1b). The ratio of master's/doctoral publications has varied widely

1 The selection of the year 2000 as a starting point for the literature searches and ensuing discussion is somewhat arbitrary, but it helps establish a baseline for comparisons with the past two decades of literature. The list of articles was not refined further for relevancy due to lack of criteria for doing so, but comparisons between groups are still appropriate as any errors associated with inappropriate inclusion should be systematic.

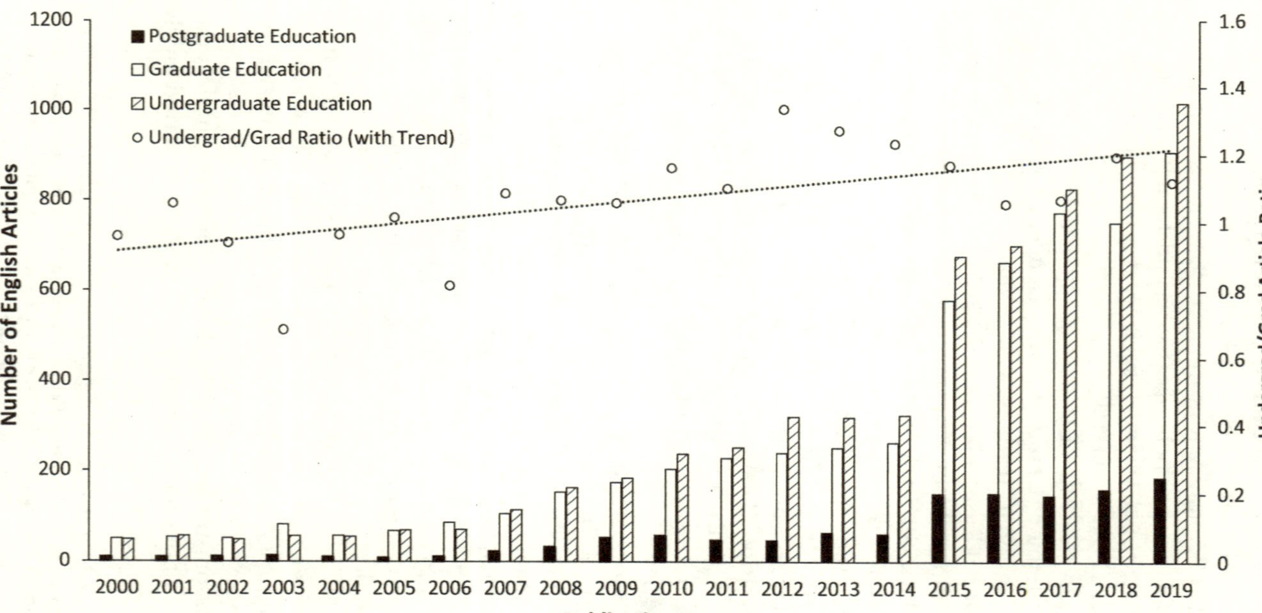

Figure 1a. A sampling of undergraduate/graduate/postgraduate education–related articles since 2000.
Note: Data are from a Web of Science (WoS) search conducted January 3, 2020, using the search terms TS = (Graduate OR Undergraduate OR Postgraduate) AND TS = (Education) AND WC = (Education & Educational Research). The search was limited to English language publications and articles. Data for 2019 may not be complete.

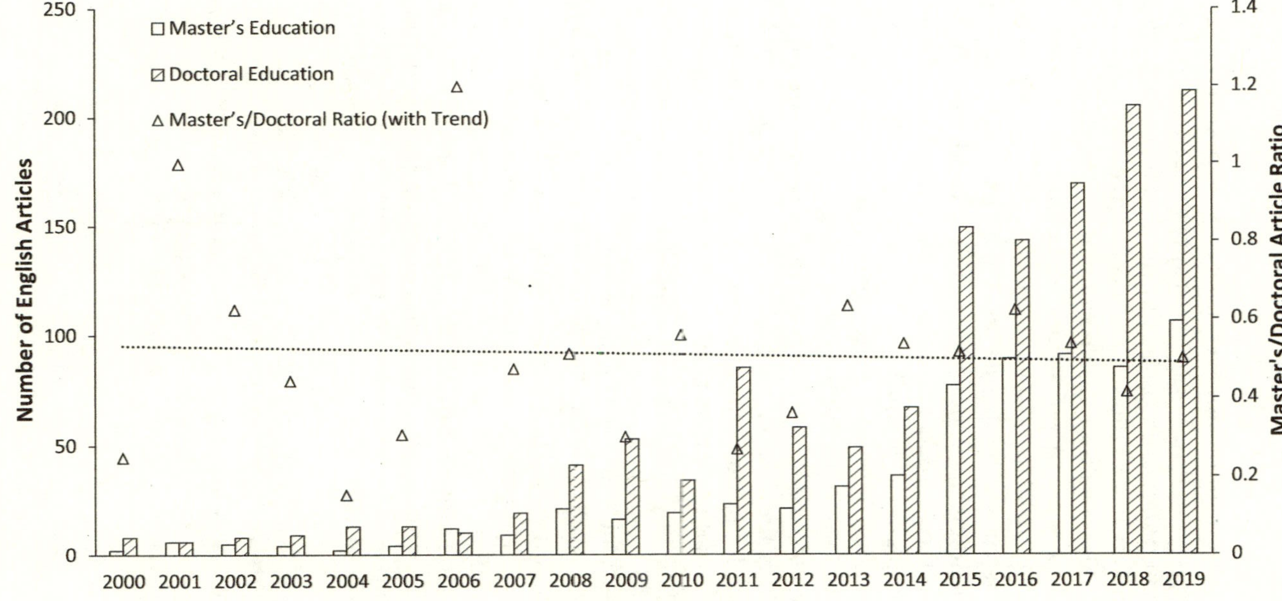

Figure 1b. A sampling of doctoral/master's education–related articles since 2000.
Note: Data are from a Web of Science (WoS) search conducted January 3, 2020, using the search terms TS = (Doctoral OR Master's) AND TS = (Education) AND WC = (Education & Educational Research). The search was limited to English language publications and articles. Data for 2019 may not be complete.

but hovers around 0.5 – two publications on doctoral education for every one on master's education. Again, research on doctoral education would appear to be relatively healthy.

Beyond the publication count, however, the range of research topics in the literature is narrow in terms of both disciplinary and geographic representation. The top four WoS "Research Area" categories (collectively representing about 10% of the sample set) for graduate education publications during this time frame (aside from the "Education and Educational Research" category to which they all belong) are business/economics, psychology, social work, and psychiatry (table 1). When the literature search is separated by degree level, the research categories change slightly depending upon how the search is conducted. If the "graduate education" literature search is simply refined by topic according to "doctoral" or "master's" identifiers, the subset of publications is relatively small (392 and 198 total over 19 years, respectively) but two (psychology and social work) of the top three categories of "Research Area" are common and change only in ordering between the two degree levels.[2] Rerunning the literature searches to specify "Doctoral Education" or "Master's Education" (as represented in figure 1b) rather than refining from "Graduate Education" yields far more publications over the same time period (1,354 and 659 respectively) but little change in the topic "Research Area" categories (table 2). The emphasis of literature at the master's level on social work is certainly understandable given its practice-oriented training. Disciplinary areas such as social work and linguistics, however, while certainly important and worthy of investigation, do not correspond to the areas in which the largest number of degrees are conferred, particularly at the doctoral level (National Center for Science and Engineering Statistics, 2019a). For example, the number of publications related to doctoral education in engineering (8) is not commensurate with the number of engineering PhDs granted in the United States (89,640) over the past 10 years alone (2009–18), which is about 30 times the number of PhDs granted in social work (3,120) or linguistics (2,585) (National Center for Science and Engineering Statistics, 2019b). As a result, there is misalignment between the peer-reviewed research being generated and the graduate degrees awarded by discipline. There is nothing to suggest that these two factors should correlate in a one-to-one manner; however, there are clearly gaps in the literature.

---

2 The doctoral and master's numbers do not sum to the total graduate education articles for any topic since these keywords may not have been used by the authors.

Table 1. Top 20 research areas of graduate education–related journal articles (2000–19, English only)

Research Area	Number of Articles
Business/Economics	187
Psychology	140
Social Work	112
Psychiatry	104
Linguistics	98
Health Care Sciences/Services	77
Social Sciences (Other Topics)	71
Sociology	64
Computer Science	60
Engineering	57
Sport Sciences	52
Geography	49
Music	44
Geriatrics/Gerontology	40
Public Environmental/Occupational Health	39
Science Technology (Other Topics)	36
Urban Studies	28
Environmental Sciences/Ecology	27
Art	21
Ethnic Studies	14

Table 2. Research areas of doctoral and master's education–related journal articles (2000–19, English only)

Doctoral Education Articles Research Areas	Number of Articles	Master's Education Articles Research Areas	Number of Articles
Sport Sciences	50	Social Work	46
Psychology	49	Linguistics	20
Social Work	41	Psychology	16
Social Sciences (Other Topics)	22	Business/Economics	13
Linguistics	18	Geography	9
Art	15	Science Technology (Other Topics)	8
Business Economics	15	Sport Sciences	8
Music	12	Health Care Sciences Services	7
Sociology	12	Geriatrics/Gerontology	6
Geography	9	Computer Science	5
Engineering	8	Urban Studies	5
Ethnic Studies	8	Music	4
Computer Science	5	Social Sciences (Other Topics)	4
Geriatrics/Gerontology	5	Engineering	3
History/Philosophy of Science	5	Art	2
Cultural Studies	4	Communication	2

Table 3. Top 10 countries of author origin for undergraduate and graduate education journal articles (2000–19, English only)

Undergraduate Education Articles			Graduate Education Articles		
Countries/Territories	Number of Articles	%	Countries/Territories	Number of Articles	%
United States	2,435	37.8	United States	2,513	43.7
England	927	14.4	Australia	691	12.0
Australia	683	10.6	England	592	10.3
Canada	342	5.3	Canada	299	5.2
China	273	4.2	China	187	3.3
Turkey	267	4.1	Turkey	180	3.1
Spain	165	2.6	South Africa	177	3.1
South Africa	156	2.4	New Zealand	107	1.9
Netherlands	130	2.0	Spain	105	1.8
Germany	129	2.0	Germany	95	1.7

The number of articles identified as relating to "postgraduate education" relative to "graduate education" (figure 1a) not only highlights the geographical differences in terminology recognized earlier but serves as the starting point for a comparison of the authors' countries of origin. Although these searches were limited to English-only articles, less than half of the results are attributable to authors based in North America (table 3). Approximately one-quarter come from Australia and England combined (roughly true at both undergraduate and graduate levels). A somewhat surprising fraction of the English-language postsecondary education articles come from Turkey and China. The number of publications becomes too small to be meaningful when the graduate education publications are refined by "doctoral" or "master's" topics but, when the *ab initio* search terms "doctoral education" and "master's education" are used as before, the geographic distribution of articles remains similar to the "graduate education" articles, especially at the doctoral level (table 4). Finally, with respect to publishers, the health sciences journals dominate both the undergraduate and graduate education literature as a whole but, when broken down by degree level, educational research journals such as *Studies in Higher Education* dominate at the doctoral level (table 5) while the discipline-based educational journals once again are home to relevant articles primarily on master's-level education.

Over nearly two decades around the world, there have been roughly 5,800 peer-reviewed journal articles devoted to graduate education, 400 to 1,400 devoted to doctoral education, and 200 to over 650 related

Table 4. Top 10 countries of author origin for doctoral and master's education journal articles (2000–19 English only)

Doctoral Education Articles			Master's Education Articles		
Countries/Territories	Number of Articles	%	Countries/Territories	Number of Articles	%
United States	573	42.3	United States	224	34.0
Australia	209	15.4	England	70	10.6
England	177	13.0	Spain	46	7.0
South Africa	64	4.7	China	28	4.2
Canada	55	4.0	Turkey	28	4.2
New Zealand	48	3.5	Netherlands	27	4.1
China	41	3.0	Norway	24	3.6
Turkey	32	2.4	Finland	23	3.5
Spain	28	2.0	South Africa	23	3.5
Sweden	26	1.9	Sweden	20	3.0

Table 5. Top 10 journals for doctoral and master's education publications (2000–19, English only)

Doctoral Education Articles			Master's Education Articles		
Source Titles	Number of Articles	%	Source Titles	Number of Articles	%
Studies in Higher Education	117	8.6	*Journal of Social Work Education*	46	7.0
Higher Education Research Development	63	4.7	*Studies in Higher Education*	19	2.9
Higher Education	60	4.4	*Assessment & Evaluation in Higher Education*	12	1.8
Innovations in Education and Teaching	45	3.3	*Higher Education*	12	1.8
International Journal of Social Work Education	41	3.0	*BMC Medical Education*	11	1.7

to master's education, depending on how one counts. That may seem like a reasonable number of publications on the subject but, when compared to the number of research publications (as also determined with a 2000–19, English-only article WoS search) in any similarly broad area of scholarship such as climate change (>236,000), gene therapy (~158,000), social media (>56,000), and globalization (>27,000) or even a narrowly defined research topic such as health disparities in Indigenous Peoples (372 journal articles in 19 years), the need for more foundational study is clear.

Presentation of Topics: A Research Agenda

How should this foundational research on graduate education be generated and who should generate it? As with most questions, there are several possible answers. Proposed here is an outline for just one approach.

This introduction began with a justification for three broad categories of research topics: the science of graduate-level learning, its usefulness for career preparation, and the need for program improvement. The reasoning is that these three areas correspond to the key constituents who can best effect change: faculty, students, and administrators. There are certainly other constituencies to consider, including employers, policy makers, and even family members, but the voice for these constituencies is provided in the context of the three broader categories. Employers, for example, should have input into career preparation and program improvement, as should policy makers. The influence of family members is considered in the discussion of student decision-making processes and success in graduate school. These three topic areas also allow the analysis to transcend disciplinary and degree-based boundaries. How can one discuss new problem-based approaches to research in the context of traditional disciplines or propose radical changes to degree structures within a master's vs. doctoral framework? These organizational approaches were purposely avoided. The three topic areas provide adequate boundaries within which to organize relevant research questions.

As for the research questions themselves, there are many ways to generate new knowledge; it is not the purpose of this monograph to review the theoretical underpinnings of research and scholarship (with the possible exception of how they apply to the training of graduate students, as discussed in chapter 1). Creative discovery and hypothesis testing are examples of two very different approaches. Both can work. Many of the early advances in graduate education were based on creative discovery. What seemed to be working at one institution led others to follow with similar graduate programs. Ideas were shared and commonalities were found. Similarly, scholarship from areas such as behavioral psychology, which has rigorous ethical constraints on human subjects research, finds its way into graduate education. For example, communities-of-practice theory has been borrowed from behavioral psychology to introduce journal clubs to engineering graduate education (Newswander & Borrego, 2009) in order to improve knowledge accumulation, problem solving, creativity, and collaboration. The recent rise in the use of individual development plans (IDPs) to enhance the career preparation of graduate students is another example of scholarship borrowed from portfolio-based approaches at lower educational levels (Manathunga & Lant, 2006). In contrast, few theories and research methods have been borrowed from the sciences and engineering to study graduate education in non-STEM disciplines such as the humanities, arts, business, or law. The primary research tool in STEM disciplines is hypothesis testing. There are certainly limitations to hypothesis testing, especially when there is insufficient theory to underpin the covariational studies (Mearsheimer & Walt, 2013), but it can be a useful tool when properly employed. A null hypothesis is posed and experiments are carried out to test it. With this approach comes the need to understand control groups, design of experiments, types of errors, and confidence limits of conclusions.

These approaches could be characterized as qualitative vs. quantitative or interpretive vs. outcomes-oriented (causal), as in the so-called paradigm wars of the educational research community (Galvez et al., 2019). It is not the purpose of this monograph to weigh the relative merits of these approaches, especially when these approaches are posed as inflexible dichotomies. It is interesting to note in the work of Galvez et al., however, that in their analysis of 137,024 dissertation titles from schools of education in the United States from 1980–2010, the terms "graduate education" and "engineering" were not included in the 60 title topic categories. This finding leads one to believe that even graduate-level educational researchers rarely engage in research on graduate education outside of their own discipline. Nevertheless, we know that there are people rigorously trained in a range of research techniques. They undoubtedly come from the educational research community but also from physics, sociology, chemical engineering, and informatics disciplines, just to name a few. When teamed with those skilled in qualitative and/or human subjects research – especially with additional disciplinary expertise – the results can be powerful. The answer to how foundational research on graduate education should be carried out, then, is partly answered by who performs it.

The arguments in this monograph are that more mixed-methods investigations in all graduate education disciplines (not just STEM) are needed, that larger and more robust data sets must be utilized, that longitudinal studies must be initiated now (because if we do not start them, we cannot finish them), and that graduate education research should be carried out by multidisciplinary teams of qualified investigators. The agenda presented here is not a collection of research hypotheses to test – the possibilities are endless; rather, it is a research outline comprising general areas of investigation that are meant to organize the panoply of research topics into manageable "buckets" that can be departure points for discussion and future projects. The topics are presented as questions, with descriptions of what is known from the literature interposed with limitations of the studies and examples of what is not known (in the form of questions) that can serve as the basis for further research. Existing theories are presented in simplified, graphical form so as to draw upon commonalities and highlight areas for testing. For example, many of the schematic figures illustrate theories that have been distilled to their most fundamental components. The original citations contain critical additional detail but, for the purposes of this research agenda, the broad concepts are most important for illuminating the key areas for testing.

The research questions that serve as section headers are purposely broad and likely ill-suited to direct investigation. They are meant as categories of research questions that, with proper narrowing and specificity, could shed significant light on parts of the graduate education enterprise that heretofore may have been surmised but not properly supported with research results. These research questions are intended equally for graduate programs as well as graduate schools, though their framing – and as a result their utility – will be different for each group. Put another way, each question could appropriately end with "... in our program," "... in our graduate school," "... at our university," or "... in North America (or any other country or region of interest)." The questions that form each section comprise key research themes for the graduate education community to pursue, with kernels of guidance from the current literature. Testable models that link factors with outcomes (e.g., the effects of summer bridge programs on underrepresented minority [URM] degree completion over a multi-year period at a cohort of institutions) are highlighted over simple descriptive statistics (e.g., X% of students completed their degree in Y amount of time in year Z at institution A in program B) or purely anecdotal descriptions (e.g., "the new lab-rotation approach to advisor selection described in this article was well received by the first cohort of graduate students") but all types of studies can in some way shape our understanding of the science of graduate-level learning, career preparation for advanced degree holders, and graduate program improvement.

1 The Science of Graduate-Level Learning

There is an ever-growing body of work on learning and teaching that has fundamentally changed how curricula are delivered inside and outside the classroom – at the undergraduate level. Active learning (Bonwell & Eison, 1991), experiential learning (Cantor, 1997), and outcomes assessment (Brookhart, 1999) are just three examples of how educational research has influenced the delivery of undergraduate curricula. Numerous additional examples provide lenses through which research on graduate student learning can be viewed. Just as at the undergraduate level, learning theories on graduate education can be developed and tested. New methods of graduate-level instruction can be taught to faculty. Graduate-level educational objectives can be defined and assessed. Such approaches are rare.

One curricular approach has been to focus solely on what students learn. Although competency-based education has recently been a prominent topic of discussion in the mainstream media (see these Huffington Post [Mendenhall, 2012] and Center for American Progress [Soares, 2012] articles, for example), it has been a well-established learning methodology in specific disciplines for quite some time (Carraccio et al., 2002). Its basic implication for graduate education is that students can master requisite skills at their own pace and progress through degree programs based on accomplishment rather than artificially imposed temporal constraints. For example, is the research mentor–mentee relationship adequately represented by a competency? More important, perhaps, is the impact of how these skills are taught and learned on how well they are retained throughout one's professional lifetime.

The common assumption is that graduate education is distinctly different from undergraduate education. Whereas the evolution of skills at the baccalaureate level is seen as more or less uniform across the degree

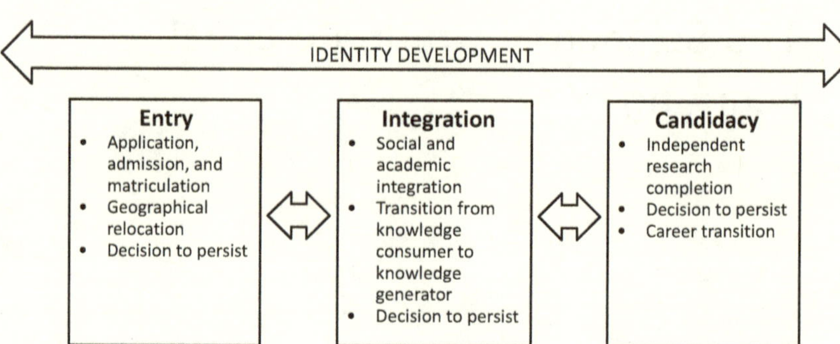

Figure 2. Development phases of doctoral candidates. Adapted from Gardner, 2009.

program (undergraduates often take liberal arts electives over all three or four years, and courses in the major include electives that can be taken at various stages), the development of skills at the graduate level falls into distinct categories, with sequential (some would say lockstep) academic milestones such as qualifying examinations, prospectuses, or admission to candidacy separating the stages. Attempts have been made to change this perception. For example, a model for doctoral student development has been proposed (Gardner, 2009) that identifies three fluid and overlapping phases: entry into the program, integration into the program, and candidacy for degree (figure 2). While the categories imply a more-or-less chronological approach to skills development, the skills, in fact, are continuously developed and refined across all phases. This adaptation of student development theory to the graduate level is useful for categorizing the phases of skills development and recognizing that skills development is neither static nor necessarily satisfied with the attainment of a specific academic goal. The theory does not, however, give us much guidance on what those skills should be, nor has it been tested to see if attrition happens at the points predicted by the model or for the reasons it suggests. Nevertheless, the concept of skills development is as useful at the graduate level as it is any other level of instruction.

So, what are exactly graduate-level skills? More importantly, what is a skill? The term "skills" is used here in the most general sense to identify those broad areas of abilities and characteristics that graduate students are expected to exhibit upon degree completion. Related terms like "competence," "abilities," and to some extent "educational objectives" can be used interchangeably. More detailed differentiation between these terms will be given later in this chapter and again in chapter 3 on graduate program improvement but, for now, the focus will be on the relationship between the "what" and "how" of graduate education and how both can be improved. Clarification of terminology, however, does not help us identify what those skills should be. It is that lack of definition of "what" that establishes the first overarching research topic on the agenda. The subsequent research questions in this section then consider the "how," including the relationship of teaching and research skills, the impact of mentoring, the effect of interdisciplinary teams, the role of online instruction, and the influence of theses and dissertations on graduate student learning. Existing models and theories are reviewed, interspersed with remaining questions that provide opportunities for further research, testing of models, and application of theory.

What Skills Must Graduate Students Attain and How Do They Best Attain Those Skills?

What graduate students are expected to know and be able to do upon degree completion are as varied as the degree names themselves and the institutions that offer them. There are surely disciplinary differences in the professional skills required for career success. An MFA in theater prepares one to do something that a PhD in materials science does not and vice versa. The research question is not really about what those specific skills should be but how those requisite career and educational skills are identified, categorized, and, most importantly, assessed. Approaches to defining what graduate students should know range from climbing further up the ladder of Bloom's taxonomy as a continuation from the undergraduate level (Granello, 2001) to the nebulous "I know it when I see it" approach often found in the PhD dissertation defense. There are more robust approaches.

One such approach is to use the terminology adopted by the National Research Council (NRC). The key skills students at any level must learn fall into three broad categories (Pellegrino & Hilton, 2013): cognitive, interpersonal, and intrapersonal. These oversimplified categories are not without controversy and there are, of course, overlapping skills for any given learning outcome. For example, critical thinking comprises both cognitive and dispositional (intrapersonal) dimensions (N. Lawrence et al., 2009). Although these three categories of skills development may be oversimplified and there are significant areas of overlap, the conversation on learning at the graduate level is at least bounded. This domain-level approach to skills identification and development will be utilized heavily throughout this monograph.

There are other approaches. In the United Kingdom, the Research Councils UK (RCUK) has defined skills training requirements for research students. Skills categories include research skills and techniques (as a distinct and separate category), research environment, research management, personal effectiveness, communication skills, networking and team working, and career management. It does not, however, give any guidance on how these skills are to be developed other than through "appropriate" techniques such as self-direction, supervisor support and mentoring, departmental support, workshops, conferences' elective training courses, formally assessed courses, and informal opportunities. Nor does it provide any assessment criteria for these activities.

Some models both classify research skills and differentiate between levels of research based on researcher autonomy. One such framework comes from the University of Adelaide (Willison & O'Regan, 2017), where a seven-level Researcher Skill Development (RSD7) model can be used to not only enumerate research skills but follow their development through various stages. This model is adapted and summarized in figure 3, with educational-level categories added for the sake of discussion solely based on this author's experiences. Several items are worthy of note and clarification. First, the educational-level categories in figure 3 are typically much broader than indicated on the diagram and are not meant to be prescriptive. In fact, most research experiences start at a much lower level and progress through stages, regardless of who is performing the research. The educational levels, then, indicate a level of research skill investigators might attain at the termination of their schooling, degree program, or research project. Second, the framers of this model note that postdoctoral scholars (postdocs) sometimes report having less autonomy than they did as PhD students and may find themselves conducting closed rather than open inquiry. This topic itself is worthy of further investigation.

The Embark & Clarify category of skills primarily encompasses hypothesis formulation, which can come from supervisor input at the Self-Initiated Research level, or from the researcher at the Open Research level. Especially at the doctoral level, an important component of hypothesis formulation is the literature review. The purpose of the literature review varies widely by field and even country. It can be viewed as justification for the research being proposed or as a scholarly work in and of itself (LeCompte et al., 2003). There are methods for evaluating the literature review, including rubrics (Boote & Beile, 2005), but little clarification on exactly what skills are fostered. What role does the literature review play in the development of a researcher? Are the skills developed during the literature review stage utilized more or less than

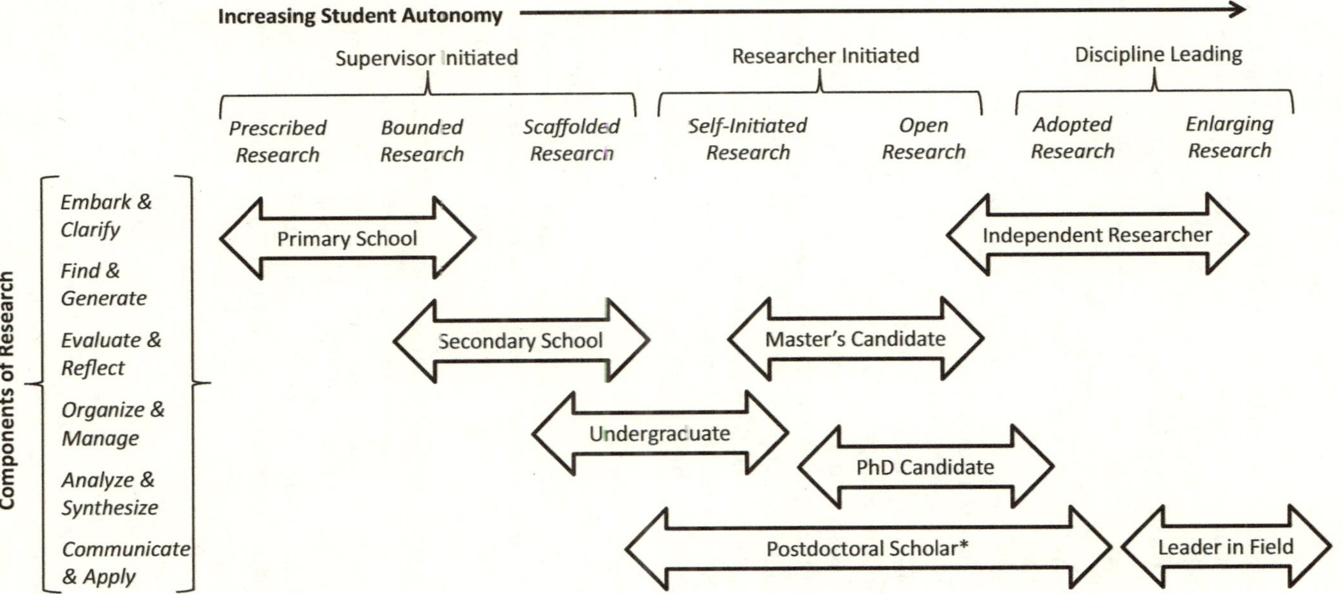

Figure 3. Seven-level Research Skill Development (RSD7) framework. Adapted from Willison & O'Regan, 2017.

* Postdoctoral scholars often report having less autonomy than they did as PhD students and may find themselves conducting closed inquiry rather than open inquiry.

other research skills after graduate school? How are literature review skills best taught?

Researchers then move to data collection in the Find & Generate stage using appropriate methods and, in some cases, developing their own. These research methods are taught in some disciplines as part of a structured curriculum, or in others on an as-needed basis through mentoring activities. What are the preferred methods of teaching research methodologies to those conducting open research? The collected information is then critiqued in the Evaluate & Reflect stage using techniques that can be taught in a similar way to (and often alongside) the methodological approaches to data collection. The remaining categories (Organize & Manage, Analyze & Synthesize, and Communicate & Apply) are where pedagogical approaches often become less structured at the master's and doctoral levels. What aspects of project management, for example, could be beneficial in these stages of research and how are they best delivered? Are the analysis and synthesis reflected in a thesis, dissertation, journal publication, or book substantive enough? How are graduate students taught to use appropriate language to communicate their findings to a variety of audiences? This framework, and others like it, can help us enumerate research skills and identify appropriate methods for their effective development. These frameworks also assist in developing research questions that span educational level and time. How do undergraduate research experiences impact specific research skills development at the graduate level? How do students who come into graduate school without previous research experience advance to the same level as those who already have such experience? What roles do such individual characteristics like self-motivation play in the long-term development of research skills?

Another way to view skills development is in terms of "signature pedagogies" that are specific to a discipline (Shulman, 2005). The health sciences community has especially embraced what they term "competencies," as in epidemiology where 11 common competencies were identified for PhD programs at 48 CEPH-accredited institutions (Hlaing, 2019). What is interesting in this study is that the competency related to conducting an advanced original research project was identified as important to a majority of PhD epidemiology programs but not to a majority of DrPH programs. Although the sample set was small, this differentiation of skills by degree type can help us understand what types of careers students are preparing for. Similarly, signature pedagogies like journal clubs from neuroscience and literature lists from English have been adapted to other fields such as educational research (Golde, 2007) but, as Golde points out, these new pedagogies must be assessed

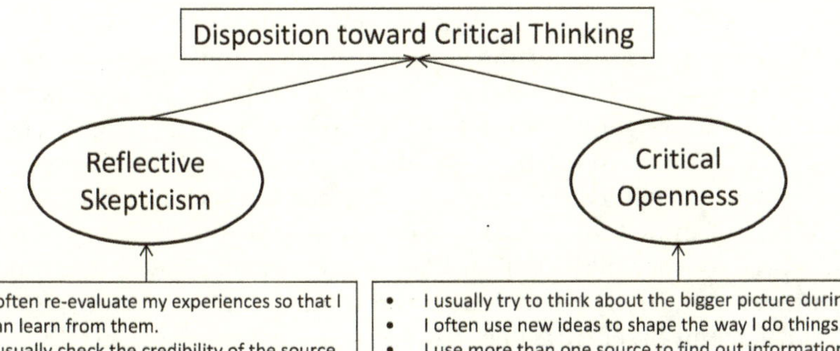

Figure 4. Two-factor confirmatory analysis (CFA) model for disposition toward critical thinking. Adapted from Sosu, 2013.

carefully and results shared. One suggestion (Feldon et al., 2010) has been to utilize rubrics to evaluate STEM doctoral-student performance. At the doctoral level, the development of research skills is a key differentiator from other graduate degrees; however, these research skills are often not clearly defined, much less assessed. This lack of structure makes it virtually impossible to measure how research skills are best learned.

Despite the lack of structure, skills development and learning at the graduate level have undergone some investigation. Within the critical thinking dimension, for example, one study from the United Kingdom (Sosu, 2013) showed that the Critical Thinking Disposition Scale model could identify key differences between undergraduate and graduate students in the two component scales of reflective skepticism and critical openness (figure 4). This 11-item instrument could be useful not only as a comparative tool but as a framework to collect longitudinal information on the development of critical thinking skills. As the items most influential to reflective skepticism and critical openness are quantified across different disciplines, how can pedagogical techniques be adapted to influence them? Can instruments that measure the effect of other factors (other than disposition) on critical thinking be developed and validated?

Skills assessment has long been a staple of medical education, where it is more commonly referred to as competency-based assessment. The fifteen core "competencies" for entering medical students are grouped similarly to the NRC categories (Association of American Medical Colleges, 2017): interpersonal, intrapersonal, thinking and reasoning, and science competence. Additional skills have been proposed for the taxonomy to make it more general for all healthcare professional fields (Englander et al., 2013). Post-medical school residencies and internships – termed "graduate medical education" – are assessed on six core skills (Accreditation Council for Graduate Medical Education, 2017): patient care and procedural skills, medical knowledge, practice-based learning and improvement, interpersonal and communication skills, professionalism, and systems-based practice. Common tools used to assess these skills include global ratings forms, portfolios, so-called 360-degree evaluations, and direct observation (Epstein, 2007; Lurie et al., 2009).

There is also much to learn in the cognitive domain of graduate education. While there is still significant debate over the age at which the brain finishes maturation (see Arain et al., 2013, for example), for the purposes of this monograph it is assumed that neurological development is still taking place in the brain of the traditionally aged graduate student (early to mid-20s). What are the implications of graduate student age and therefore cognitive and behavioral development to student learning? How do learning styles change – if at all – over time for individuals, or as they move from content-based study to research-based inquiry? Little is currently known.

One recent international journal issue was devoted to aspects of how doctoral students learn (Keefer et al., 2015), ranging from the crossing of conceptual thresholds such as the dissertation literature review (Wisker, 2015) to learning about disciplinary theory (Holbrook et al., 2015). In the engineering community, the Research Student Virtual Portfolio (RSVP) model has been applied to a small sample of PhD students at one Australian research university (Manathunga & Lant, 2006). They studied the outcomes of eight research graduate attributes including research, project management, and communication skills in an attempt to elucidate the factors affecting student learning and career development in interdisciplinary environments. Although this study shows a positive influence of such training activities as IDPs and structured mentoring on skills development, the results rely heavily on student self-reporting through surveys and do not provide a correlative model to assess the relative effectiveness of individual activities on attribute development. A more recent work, in contrast, utilized a mixed-methods approach to study skills development in STEM graduate students (Feldon et al., 2016). They found that skill inequality differs from other forms of inequality such as socioeconomic status or gender. The implications of this work are that pre–graduate school training, such as summer transition programs, may be instrumental in reducing the skills gap and that efforts to reduce the skills gap may extend all the way back to elementary and secondary education. A relevant review of the current literature on doctoral learning and the broadest transnational (albeit small in scale) survey of doctoral students using sociocultural theory (Hopwood, 2010) illustrate the importance of experiential learning and sociocultural engagement in enhancing the doctoral experience, especially in the area of professional skills development.

Finally, what are the interactions between the various skills domains? The relationship between intrapersonal skills, such as emotional intelligence, and academic performance has been investigated in public-administration graduate students (Jaeger, 2003). Not only was a positive correlation found between the two but it was found that emotional intelligence could be positively influenced in the classroom. This study, however, involved a sample of only 158 students in one public-administration course at a single, large, private university in the United States. The methodological details aside, how can studies like this be broadened to include a larger set of participants across multiple disciplines and institutions? What are the linkages between other skills domains and how can they be improved?

Many questions remain regarding the definition, development, and delivery of graduate-level skills, especially for the doctorate. Can the development of research methods in the PhD be transitioned to self-paced and/or electronic delivery? Which skills are foundational to research degrees and which skills (e.g., project management) are common to all graduate degrees? What is the appropriate relationship between learning outcomes and skills for master's degrees? For doctoral degrees? Is the development of an individual as an independent scholar itself a competency? Are these skills maintained and enhanced throughout one's professional career? Further complicating the competency-based approach is the fact that doctoral degree programs are primarily open-ended with typical but certainly not mandatory times to degree, suggesting that the demonstration of independent scholarship is itself a competency or skill. What would the re-envisioning of a doctoral degree as a set of demonstrable skills mean to the Humboldtian ideal of the doctorate? How are doctoral skills differentiated from those at the master's level? How do students who are required to complete their doctorates in four years compare in terms of productivity and career success relative to those who are given no such time constraints? These are not merely 18th-century salon topics. They are alternative strategies to attaining an advanced degree that must be tested and compared.

The pockets of research on graduate student learning that exist are often limited to specific disciplines, purely anecdotal descriptions, or countries where degree programs can differ widely in structure, duration, and purpose, not to mention student profiles. How can these examples be expanded and adapted to account for disciplinary, cultural, and personal differences between students and across programs? Such studies will require unprecedented levels of institutional and disciplinary cooperation as well as funding mechanisms to support the work. These topics will be addressed in the conclusion to this monograph.

The great irony in studying how graduate students best attain and retain advanced skills is that many of these students had some form of financial support and even classroom experience as a teaching assistant; some of them will be immediately thrust into academic positions with essentially autonomous teaching responsibilities. Even the vast majority of these students who do not enter academia will be faced with instructional and mentoring opportunities regardless of career choice. Did their training as researchers and scholars adequately prepare them for this enormous responsibility? At least in the discipline of economics, one recent study found that fewer than half of the new faculty respondents who obtained their PhD from the top 30 programs felt that their graduate school experience adequately prepared them to teach; nearly a quarter did not feel prepared (Allgood et al., 2018); yet 90% of the economics department chairs participating in this study stated that promotion and tenure decisions were based primarily on research productivity and that teaching performance need only be "adequate." Another recent study of economics PhD recipients entering academia found that teaching experience in graduate school had a significantly positive impact on job placement only at mid-tier-and-below–ranked institutions and actually had a negative effect on placement at top-ranked economics departments (Sullivan et al., 2018). This tension between teaching and research – particularly as it relates to skills development and graduate-level learning – is certainly not unique to the discipline of economics, so it is the topic of the next research question.

How Is the Development of Teaching and Research Skills Related?

Foundational to the graduate education enterprise is the implicit assumption that the development of research skills imbues one with the necessary expertise to teach at the postsecondary level. Why else would college and university accrediting agencies explicitly require an earned doctorate or master's degree in the discipline to teach at the baccalaureate level (see, for example, *Faculty Credentials Guidelines* for the Southern Association of Colleges and Schools Commission on Colleges, 2018)? Beyond minimum credentials for accreditation purposes, what research university does not tout the scholarly accomplishments of its faculty as a key reason for attracting prospective undergraduate and graduate students? This tenuous linkage between quantifiable metrics such as faculty scholarly productivity and student course evaluations serves as a proxy measure for the quality of the educational experience and is a key component of university ranking systems (Shin et al., 2011). The reasons for this linkage between scholarly productivity and teaching effectiveness and the resulting faculty credentialing requirements are historic (J. Robertson & Bond, 2005) and pragmatic (see Walker et al., 2008, chapter 2, for example) and have led to professional development programs aimed at improving teaching skills in graduate students, such as the Preparing Future Faculty (Gaff, 2002; Gaff et al., 2003) and Future Academic Scholars in Teaching (Prevost et al., 2018) programs. The effectiveness of such programs and the true impact that highly productive scholars have on the attainment of educational outcomes for the students they teach are certainly topics worthy of investigation. The dual role of graduate students as both emerging scholars and teachers provides key research questions from a science of learning standpoint. Does the development of research skills prepare one to be a better teacher of advanced concepts in the field? Does a focus on developing teaching skills in concert with research skills have a complementary effect? How do we best prepare graduate students to be effective teachers regardless of their career choice?

Recently, evidence for a synergistic relationship between teaching opportunities and the development of research skills has emerged. The foundation for this synergy lies in the presumption that both skill sets require similar cognitive processes. Nevertheless, the teaching assistantship is often thought of as a funding mechanism rather than a skills-development opportunity; the research suggests otherwise. Connolly et al. (2016) performed a longitudinal study of over 3,000 doctoral STEM students at three US research universities who participated in teaching development programs. Among other findings, Connolly et al. found that engaging in even one formal teaching development course had a positive impact on both short- and long-term outcomes, primarily related to self-efficacy beliefs. They also found that participation in teaching development activities did not increase time to degree – as is often a concern among faculty advisors – but that participation in actual teaching activities did increase time to degree commensurate with the time dedicated to teaching. In a related study (Shortlidge & Eddy, 2018), graduate students in the life sciences self-reported that training in evidence-based teaching positively impacted their ability to communicate scientific research and preparedness for a research career while not negatively affecting research productivity. Feldon et al. (2011) found a more direct relationship between the development of teaching and research skills in STEM graduate students. They studied the written research proposals of 95 early-career graduate students at three research universities in the United States for improvements over time in several research skills, including generating valid research designs. They found statistically significant improvement in the experimental design quality of students with both research and teaching experiences over those with research experiences alone. Similar results were found for the ability to generate testable research hypotheses. What is significant about this study is that it relied upon a defined set of research skills and itself utilized a null-hypothesis testing approach to determine differences in those skills relative to a control group. We as the graduate education community can (and should) argue about what those research and teaching skills should be and rely upon qualitative studies and self-reported assessments to help frame our conversations; however, hypothesis-based studies such as this will ultimately give us the hard evidence we need to make programmatic changes. As with any studies, however, these two examples raise more questions than they answer.

Which specific research skills do teaching experiences impact the most? Conversely, do research skills impact teaching effectiveness? What is the appropriate balance of time allotment in order to attain optimal benefit from a teaching experience while not negatively impacting the development of other research skills? At what point or points in the graduate school experience are the benefits of teaching experiences most impactful and how long should those assignments last? What are appropriate self-assessment tools that allow students to reflect upon the meaning of teaching experiences in real time?

Regardless of their future roles as teachers and educators, the primary purpose of doctoral education for the graduate student today is the development of research skills. Although some of these skills can be developed through didactic training, the majority of them are the result of the experiential approach to doctoral training: research mentorship. The next research topic focuses on graduate student learning that can be done at the individual level and is chiefly related to the advisor–advisee relationship that is the foundation of many graduate-level degree programs.

How Are Graduate Mentoring Models Changing?

This is the first research question for which the distinction between master's- and doctoral-level training becomes clearly important. Master's students need mentoring just like doctoral students do but it can take on different forms. Students in master's programs with a research product such as a thesis may have a mentoring experience similar to that of the doctoral students across the lab bench or library carrel. Those in MBA or LLM programs, on the other hand, may have quite different mentoring relationships from their doctoral DBA or JD counterparts. Even within a specific degree, the instructor-student relationship can vary by lecture format (the part-time, full-time, and executive-level variations of the MBA come to mind) and by online vs. in-person delivery. This discussion is structured around the different types of mentoring that graduate students may experience regardless of advanced degree level, with consideration given to degree format where appropriate.

Many different mentor–mentee models exist (peer to peer, group mentoring); there are even curricula devoted to practices in research mentoring (Pfund et al., 2013). There are also alternative theories of which aspects of graduate training are best delivered through one-on-one mentoring and which are better delivered by related activities such as professional socialization (Austin, 2002; Austin et al., 2009; Weidman et al., 2001; Weidman & Stein, 2003) and communities of practice (Nerad, 2012) (see the second research question in chapter 3). Regardless of the model, most of the available literature on mentoring is either anecdotal (that is, "Here is what we do and here's some proof that it works"), highly specific to the discipline (O. Davis & Nakamura, 2010) or institution (A. Lee, 2008), or both. A recent study at a research-intensive university in the United Kingdom (Turner, 2015) that provided supervisor (mentor) vignettes of four early-career academics falls into all of these categories. It used journey plots (Mille & Brimicombe, 2004) to identify key areas of challenge: supervisor expectations, student-mentor relationships, and supervisor commitment. This study is clearly from the early-career academic supervisor viewpoint; while it identifies key challenges to supervisors it does not propose how to overcome them nor are the results generalizable to all disciplines or advisor career stages. It does, however, consider both individual advisor and co-advisor mentoring relationships, which are discussed below. Can journey plots be quantified or generalized? Do journey plots conform to the categories provided in a student socialization model?

Some attempts have been made to develop quantitative instruments for evaluating the effectiveness of advisor-advisee relationships. The Reflective Supervisor Questionnaire (RSQ) (Pearson & Kayrooz, 2004) tested 58 common advisor activities in five categories or constructs as predictors of advisee satisfaction: expert coaching, facilitating the advisee, mentoring, sponsoring, and reflective practice. Through an analysis of the survey delivered to 314 (mostly doctoral) students at two research-intensive Australian universities, all but the reflective-practice construct were validated. A similar study (Aliet al., 2016) utilized 30 Likert-scale statements administered to 131 graduate student researchers and 77 supervisors at an English university to determine three categories of effective supervision: leadership, knowledge, and support. How do these models fare when applied to larger groups of students across multiple disciplines and institutions? Are mentoring relationships fundamentally different by discipline and, if so, in what respects? Feldon et al. (2015) used a mixed-methods approach to investigate the strength of research skills development in graduate students in selected STEM disciplines. They found that mentors' perceptions of their mentees' research skills do not generally match the self-evaluations by the mentees. How can these skill gaps be narrowed and what might be missing in a student's preparation for graduate school? Are advisor's expectations of mentee's research skills even realistic?

These models, and others like them, may confirm what is assumed about effective mentoring and supervision but are based on the traditional advisor-advisee dyad and do not consider emerging mentoring models such as team mentorship or cascading mentorship. Cascading mentorship occurs primarily (though not exclusively) in the laboratory-based disciplines when senior graduate students and postdocs actively participate in group discussions with junior members, even in an informal manner. A recent longitudinal study of 335 PhD students in the biological sciences in the United States showed that cascading mentorship activities were the primary factor in the skills development of junior group members (Feldon et al., 2019). Specifically, postdocs were found to enhance disproportionately the training of doctoral students regardless of their formal role as mentors. That enhancement of skills development comes in the forms of hands-on instruction, professional and academic feedback, modeling of academic careers, and emotional support. These findings shatter the illusion of the single faculty member apprenticeship model as the ideal mode for research skills development, at least in the laboratory-based biological sciences. Would postdoc mentorship training enhance this effect? One recent study suggests that it would (Hund et al., 2018). Are graduate students in small laboratory settings automatically at a disadvantage in terms of research skills development and ultimately career success? If the faculty advisor is not the key influencer of research skills development in laboratory-based disciplines, then what is the faculty advisor's role? Are the findings of research skills development in laboratory-based disciplines even relevant to the humanities and social sciences where one-on-one interaction is

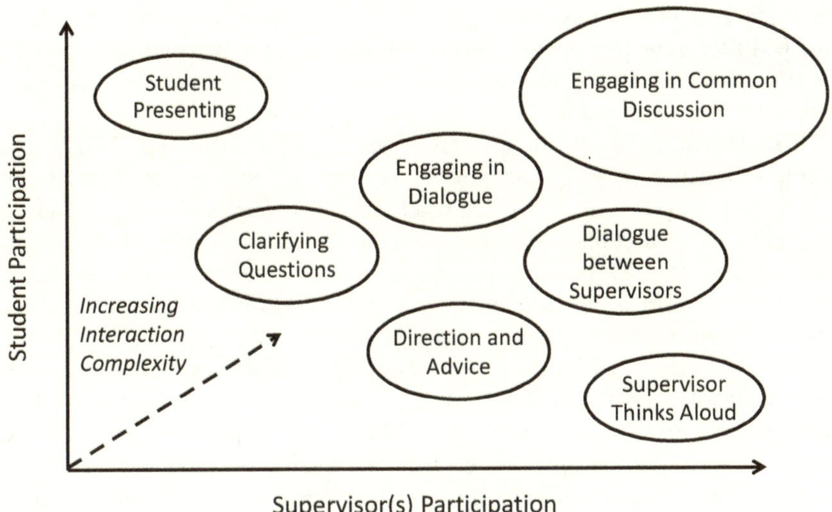

Figure 5. Complexity of mentoring interactions by participation level. Adapted from Kobayashi et al., 2015.

more common, if not the norm? What effect does supplementing the single-advisor model with even one additional mentor have on skills development in the graduate mentees?

The impact of multiple supervisors is the subject of another recent study (Kobayashi, Grout, & Rump, 2015) involving doctoral students at a major Danish university. It utilized participation and positioning theory alongside variation theory to conclude that despite the added logistical complexities, multiple supervisors can add value to the doctoral experience but only if the interaction among supervisors themselves is positive (figure 5). What factors influence co-advisor relationships? What role does the interdisciplinary nature of the research topic play in the necessity or even desirability of a co-mentor?

While useful, the results of these studies do not adequately address the effects of student variability and personality. There is a new albeit small body of literature emerging on the mentoring relationships of URM graduate students. There is an entire research question devoted to the career development needs of underrepresented students in chapter 3 but, in terms of the mentor–mentee relationship, recent articles have focused on the mentoring needs of Latinx students (Acevedo-Gil & Madrigal-Garcia, 2018; Mireles-Rios & Garcia, 2019), women in STEM (Pezzoni et al., 2016), and Black women in doctoral programs (Rasheem et al., 2018). The discussion of persistence and attrition later in this chapter will illustrate that student attitudes and personality play key roles in many aspects of the graduate school experience. The relationship with mentors is no exception.

To address these unique aspects of each student, the use of IDPs and similar mentoring tools for career advising are emerging. The use of such tools impacts many of the research questions posed here, including professional skills development and career success evaluation, but at its heart, the IDP is intended to stimulate dialogue between graduate students and their mentor(s) and advisor(s) on how best to achieve their current career goals. The interest in IDPs for graduate students has grown from the postdoctoral researcher community, especially through the NIH policy on the use of IDPs (National Institutes of Health, 2014), which strongly encourages the use of IDPs and requires a section in all research grant annual reports on how IDPs are used. NSF recently instituted a similar but less stringent requirement with its mandatory postdoctoral researcher mentoring plan on grant applications (National Science Foundation, 2015). Both funding agencies have stopped short of requiring IDPs for all graduate students funded on all grants. The argument against doing so is generally based on the added administrative burden it could present to grant principal investigators who typically also serve as research advisors. The IDP was developed as a tool for and by the advisee; viewed as such it should not present substantial additional effort on the advisor's part. Missing from this discussion is hard evidence on the potential benefits to students that IDPs might provide. Online resources exist for graduate students to develop their own IDPs (Stanford University, 2016; University of Wisconsin, 2013) irrespective of whether IDPs are required by their advisor, program, or graduate school. The graduate education community would greatly benefit from published analyses of IDP utilization, benefits, and downfalls. How do graduate students who use IDPs as part of a structured mentoring program benefit from their use? What are the most effective strategies for increasing the use of IDPs? Must they be mandated by graduate schools and/or funding agencies, or are positive results and student demand sufficient to stimulate their acceptance? Comparative studies of those who are mandated to use IDPs, those who do so voluntarily, and those who do not use IDPs at all and their resulting career success (in terms of either initial appointments or long-term leadership positions) would give preliminary evidence on the effectiveness of IDPs as career-planning tools.

The mentor–mentee relationship with all of its possible variations lies at the core of the apprenticeship-based model of research degrees. We have seen that cascading mentorship in large laboratory groups impacts graduate student skills development and that multiple mentors can have beneficial effects. These findings serve as a baseline for future studies as interdisciplinarity and team-based research become more common. As the nature of the research that graduate students are performing evolves, so must the structure of the learning environment. These are the topics of the next research question.

How Do Interdisciplinary Teams and Degree Programs Impact Graduate Student Learning?

Team-based problem solving, inquiry, and research have become popular pedagogical approaches at all levels of instruction. From the earliest educational levels, students are encouraged to share their thoughts and ideas and learn from each other's successes and mistakes. More recent pedagogical techniques such as active learning (Prince, 2004) and the flipped classroom (Abeysekera & Dawson, 2015) have components that are designed to enhance student learning through group interaction. The team-oriented approach has found its way into many undergraduate degree programs and curricula well beyond the laboratory course setting. There is an extensive body of educational research literature devoted to the team-based approach to skills development but less exists at the graduate level. Presumably many of the leading models and theories on group-based learning are extensible to graduate-level concepts – an assumption worth testing. Some evidence from the health sciences community (Sisk, 2011) suggests that they are extensible but that even there more research is required. More unique to graduate-level training with respect to team-based learning and problem solving is the research component of many graduate degrees, especially the doctorate. The opportunities for investigation of team-based research are first described; then the specific case of interdisciplinary team-based research is explored.

As described in the previous section on mentoring models, there are certainly ways in which the mentor–mentee dyad can be extended to include multiple mentors. Approaches like tiered or cascading mentorship (Feldon et al., 2019; Fowler & Muckert, 2004), where students simultaneously serve as mentors and mentees, and mutual mentoring (Sorcinelli et al., 2016) for pre-tenure faculty have been implemented but such team-based mentoring schemes do not translate necessarily into or derive from team-based research. The research component of graduate students' training is still viewed as a highly individualized effort, especially within the context of their development as independent scholars for doctoral degrees. How to evaluate the individual efforts of transdisciplinary research is a separate topic that will be described under the research question on how theses and dissertations are changing. The working premise in this section is that these individual research skills can be developed and enhanced even through team-based approaches to research. The central research question, then, is whether a team-based approach to conducting research leads to better research skills development for the individual participants. Whether team-based research leads to better research results is a wholly separate (but equally important) research topic. The evidence for or against team-based research as a skills-development tool at the graduate level is sparse but growing and is primarily qualitative. In one study of students participating in an ecological, team-based research program, three personal characteristics that contributed to overall success of the research group were identified (Nielsen-Pincus et al., 2007): vision, dedication, and problem solving. The concept of individual vision is related to risk taking, creativity, and flexibility, whereas dedication is related to commitment, professionalism, and patience. In the context of this study, problem solving relates more to conflict management and communication than it does to the ability to solve a technical problem. This study is a "lessons-learned" approach to investigating the impact of personal qualities on team-based research but it does not evaluate the reverse impact that team-based research can have on the individual. Nor is it in any way a comparative study with non–team-based research. One European study (Bruce et al., 2004) reinforces the importance of creativity, flexibility, and adaptability to team-based research but provides no empirical evidence that these skills are enhanced through participation in collaborative projects.

More recent articles have reported on longitudinal studies in selected disciplines to measure the influence of transdisciplinary research teams on student development. In a five-year study of 13 students enrolled in a joint PhD and Master's of Public Health (MPH) program at a major public research university in the United States (Keck et al., 2017), several common outcomes categorized as either benefits or barriers to transdisciplinary research were identified. Benefits identified by students included broadened networking, more learning opportunities, and increased guidance from faculty, whereas barriers included increased time commitments and unclear expectations. Participating faculty advisors identified similar benefits and barriers as well as some specific to their own professional development. The interesting longitudinal aspect of this study is that certain barriers and benefits identified by both faculty and student participants early in the study (baseline) did not persist until year five. Furthermore, many of the barriers and benefits are similar to those identified by students who are not part of transdisciplinary research teams. So, what is new and different about skills development in team environments? How does the team-based research experience impact graduate student learning and skills development? What is the interaction among interpersonal, intrapersonal, and cognitive skills development in a disciplinary team-based environment? What levels of complexity does the introduction of interdisciplinary research impart to these interactions?

Interdisciplinarity, transdisciplinarity, and cross- or multidisciplinary training are pervasive themes at most institutions and within disciplines.[3] These interrelated approaches to research are being formalized in graduate programs out of a desire to train students to tackle complex, interrelated, cross-disciplinary problems at present related to such topics as health, the environment, and the human condition. In fact, funding agencies encourage and reward interdisciplinary approaches to research. University research centers have long been funded to concentrate faculty expertise on important disciplinary-based projects. They are still much in vogue but they now tend to be multi-institutional efforts targeted at broad, interdisciplinary themes. As of 2020, for example, cross-cutting research themes at the US National Science Foundation included exploring the universe at all scales, protecting human health, and understanding the food/energy/water ecosystem. These so-called grand challenges fall under the larger umbrella of convergence research. Convergence research seeks to focus research efforts on solving complex problems based in societal need. The National Institutes of Health also funds cross-disciplinary research on the brain and has a funding instrument dedicated solely to the support of trans-institute challenges in biomedical research. The Andrew W. Mellon Foundation funds research projects in multiple countries related to such interdisciplinary topics as urbanism and diversity. The Gates Foundation focuses its funding efforts on projects at the interface of the health sciences and international development. Similar cross-disciplinary funding programs are available around the world through the Research Councils UK, Deutsche Forschungsgemeinschaft (DFG, German Research Foundation), and Australian Research Council, just to name a few. Many of the interdisciplinary research themes are common across the nations and come from reports produced by leading groups of scholars such as the US National Research Council (National Research Council, 2010, 2014a) and "grand challenges" formulated by academies, professional

3 It is beyond the scope of this text to fully define and differentiate between these four (or more) types of research collaborations that cross disciplinary boundaries. The term "interdisciplinary" will be used here in its broadest sense to include these various types of approaches to training and research.

societies (National Academy of Engineering, 2016; Uehara et al., 2013), and governmental agencies (OECD Publishing, 2010).

These funding opportunities have, in turn, led to the establishment of research training groups (RTGs). The NSF Integrative Graduate Education and Research Traineeship (IGERT, now National Research Traineeship, NRT) and recently completed NIH Broadening Experiences in Scientific Training (BEST) programs are examples in the United States of RTG funding mechanisms in the sciences and engineering. The RTG need not be interdisciplinary but it often is. It also increasingly contains an international component through student exchanges, lab rotations, or fixed-term international research stays. The German Research Foundation (DFG) has been particularly interested in the experiences of researchers in their RTGs and international RTGs (Heidler, 2015) but the long-term benefits to student participants are largely unknown.

The barriers to and potential benefits of these interdisciplinary collaborations have been well documented, dating back to well before the recent funding emphasis (Eigenbrode et al., 2007; Golde & Gallagher, 1999). That ongoing discussion need not be summarized here. What is relevant to the current research topic on group-based training of graduate students is the effect that both the group-based dynamics and the interdisciplinary components of the research have on learning and ultimately career preparation. A common concern coming from the participating disciplines is the extent to which disciplinary expertise is being sacrificed for cross-disciplinary skill; that is, the depth-vs.-breadth debate. A related concern is the impact interdisciplinary degrees can have on employability, especially in academia where disciplinary silos are still heavily ensconced. Although the impact of interdisciplinary training is an emerging area of scholarship, systematic studies have yet to be performed on the career impact of interdisciplinary preparation of graduate students. Luckily, some early program assessments that can help guide the formative aspects of group-based research activities are finding their way into the literature.

The first group of evaluations and studies from the NSF IGERT programs outlines the benefits to participants and institutions as well as identifies ways to overcome common concerns such as disciplinary-based areas of emphasis and certificates (Van Hartesveldt & Giordan, 2008). The learning outcomes enumerated by the funded IGERT programs have been compared with similar efforts in the humanities (Borrego & Newswander, 2010). The categories of learning outcomes are generally similar across these disciplines, with teamwork identified as the most common learning outcome in the science and engineering interdisciplinary group programs. A broader study of four IGERT programs focused on student socialization (Boden et al., 2011). They found that such institutional barriers as space allocation and departmental affiliations of faculty advisors can affect graduate student socialization in interdisciplinary research groups. What effect these programmatic barriers have on student learning is still an open question. These structural and social conditions were also explored in one study from Australia on interdisciplinary research groups in ecology (Buizer et al., 2015), in which activities such as joint fieldwork and joint publications were not only measurable outcomes of interdisciplinary group research but factors that could positively influence student socialization. A more detailed model on cross-training graduate students in environmental research has emerged (Schmidt et al., 2012). These investigators liken the crossing of conceptual boundaries to the crossing of physical ones. This so-called I^3 approach identifies the interdisciplinary, interorganizational, and international borders as requiring common, transferable skills. They report primarily on the programmatic aspects of I^3 training; no comparative results on its efficacy have been published to date. One publication gives graduate students' perspectives on interdisciplinary training and points to the importance of finding an "intellectual home" regardless of its disciplinary affiliation (Graybill et al., 2006). Finally, one of the few quantitative impact studies of interdisciplinary training focused solely on salary (Hanks & Kniffin, 2014). It found no influence of completing an interdisciplinary dissertation on salary within an employment sector. In a follow-on study (Kniffin & Hanks, 2018), however, these same researchers found that working in teams as a PhD holder did indeed carry a salary premium, although teamwork-based employment also required more time working.

The implications of these investigations on funding policies should not be underestimated. Funding mechanisms to support interdisciplinary research teams came from expert reports cited earlier that outlined key needs and grand challenges. In order for the interdisciplinary training group research approach to continue and thrive, there will need to be carefully crafted, longitudinal studies that enumerate the career benefits of participating in true interdisciplinary group-based research. What are the specific skills that students develop through interdisciplinary group-based research that those who participate in disciplinary-based group research or individual disciplinary research do not? What are the effects of international experiences on interdisciplinary skills development? How does team-based training impact individual accountability and subsequent career success?

Comparative studies on interdisciplinarity and team-based research can be carried out within institutions, between consortia of institutions with similar missions, or across institutions funded through such mechanisms as center-based research grants. These are subjects for the conclusion of this monograph. What has been missing in the discussion up to this point, however, is the impact on graduate student learning of an evolving learning environment: the virtual world. This topic is addressed next.

How Will (or Do) Online Instruction and Distance Education Impact Graduate Student Learning?

Residing perhaps at the opposite end of the learning styles spectrum from interdisciplinary team-based inquiry, and not wholly unrelated to the issues of professional skills development and competency-based education, is the use of online instruction – in both synchronous and asynchronous forms – and distance education for content delivery. Little is known about the efficacy of distance education in graduate education, much less specifically for doctoral degrees. Data from the fall 2018 Integrated Postsecondary Education Data System (IPEDS) survey (Department of Education, 2020) show that of the over 3 million US students taking graduate-level courses, 31% were enrolled exclusively in distance education courses. These values have changed in some significant ways over the preceding six years (figure 6) but there are also some consistencies. It is well-known that for-profit private institutions rely heavily on distance courses for their educational programs; however, the number of students enrolled in exclusively distance courses has been in decline at for-profit institutions since 2016. Not-for-profit institutions (both public and private) have seen increases in enrollments in distance education courses at the graduate level, with public institutions leading not only in absolute numbers but also in the rate of increase. These trends in distance education enrollments are superimposed upon the slow but steady growth in graduate enrollment nationwide.

When grouped by institutional mission as reflected in the Carnegie basic classification system (figure 7), the "Very High Research" institutions have the lowest percentage of graduate students enrolled only in distance education courses. Somewhat surprising, perhaps, is that smaller master's-level institutions rely less on graduate-level distance courses than do doctoral/professional universities, which have the highest percentage of students enrolled in graduate-level distance courses. The IPEDS data provide no information about the degree-seeking status of students taking online graduate-level courses and demographic data is limited to what IPEDS collects. IPEDS provides a breakdown of online enrollment by in-state and out-of-state status, however, which indicates a higher percentage of students taking online graduate-level courses outside their home state in comparison to those at the undergraduate level.

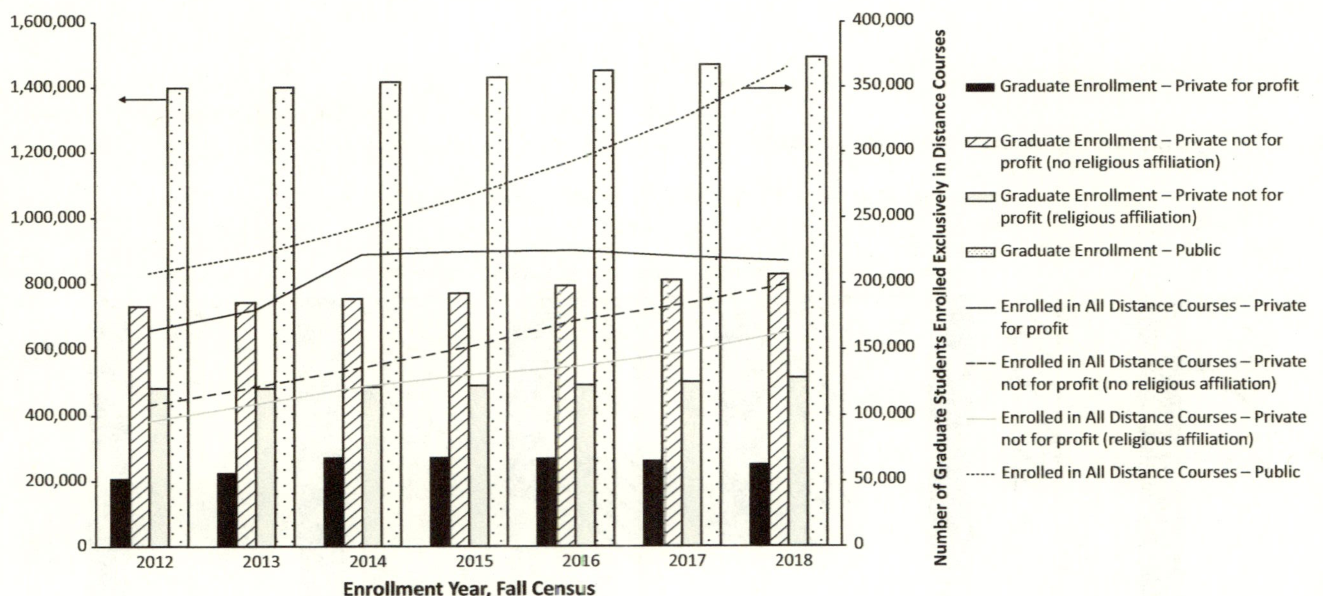

Figure 6. Total graduate students enrolled and those enrolled only in distance courses by institutional affiliation since 2012. Source: IPEDS (Department of Education, 2020).

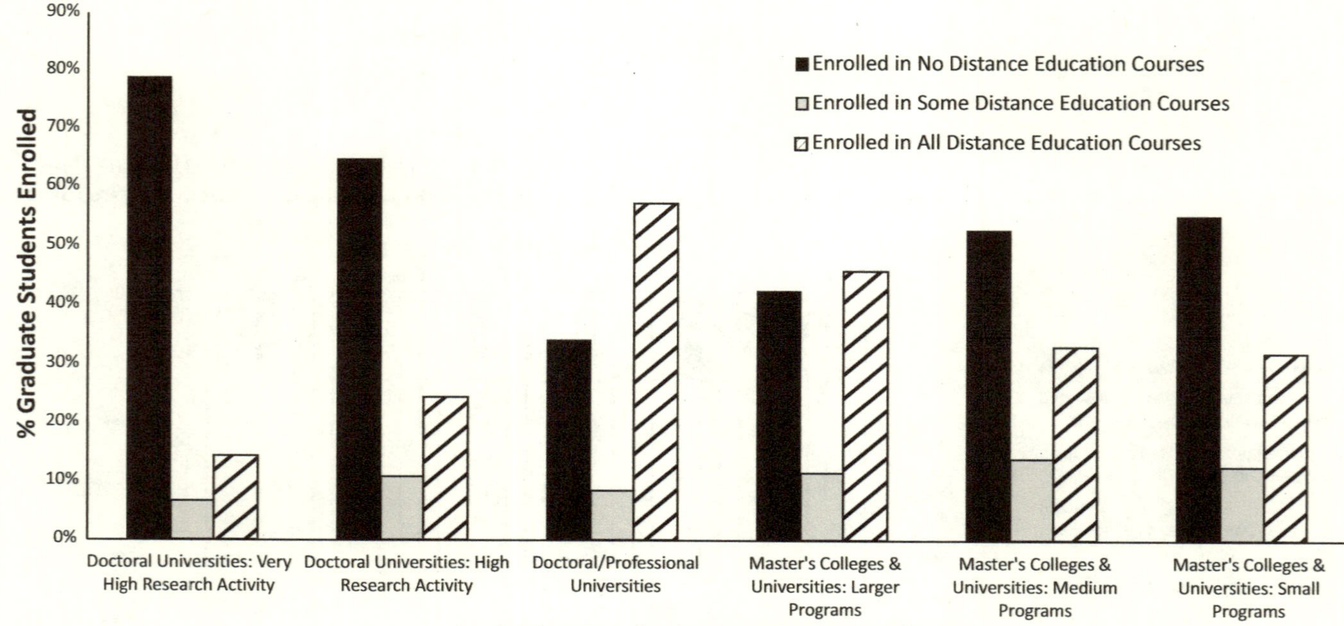

Figure 7. Percentage of graduate students enrolled in distance courses by Carnegie basic classification. Source: IPEDS provisional fall 2018 data (Department of Education, 2020).

Beyond these statistics, there is even more to learn on the pedagogical utility of distance education and online instruction at the graduate level. If one is of the opinion that a graduate degree can be distilled down to learning a discrete set of skills, then the potential exists to learn at least a subset of those skills through digital delivery. The use of asynchronous online instruction is by no means new to graduate education, particularly in the health sciences (Colley et al., 2019) and social work (Cummings et al., 2019). These disciplines also put much effort into determining how best to recruit students into these programs and in evaluating their effectiveness for professional accreditation. Those are the subjects of chapters 2 and 3 respectively. But in terms of the topic at hand – student learning – little is known about the online approach at the graduate level.

Studies evaluating the efficacy of online instruction on skills development range from the robust, such as the previously cited master's-level healthcare education, to the paltry, such as online PhD programs. In the case of the latter, much work remains to be done. One study utilized the Research Self-Efficacy Scale to evaluate the experiences of online doctoral students in their first "core research" course (Baltes et al., 2010). Self-efficacy is a learner's belief in their ability to execute the necessary courses of action to succeed (Bandura, 1997). The Baltes study showed a decrease in overall student self-efficacy in the area of research implementation from the beginning of the course to the end; however, that study was severely hampered by low response rates and limited to online doctoral students at only one institution. A more recent but similar study with adult online learners in a master's of science degree program in computing at a large, public institution found that students with prior online learning experiences had lower learning self-efficacy (Kreth et al., 2019). They postulate that self-efficacy may limit a graduate student's ability to succeed in online programs. They also found gender variation in levels of self-efficacy. The roles of gender, race, and academic discipline on graduate-level learning were the subject of one study at a health, human services, and law university in the Eastern United States (Owens & Lilly, 2017). They used web-use skills as a proxy for actual skills and found that gender and race had the strongest influence on web-use skills among the participants. There were disciplinary variations that could not be explained by gender and race, however. They, too, cite self-efficacy as a factor influencing web-use skills in their professional student population.

If self-efficacy is a key contributor to success in an online learning environment, then what does this mean for the research skills development component of advanced degrees? How do the research skills of students from online doctoral programs compare with those of students from traditional or hybrid doctoral programs? How do variations in format – not just online vs. in person but executive format (weekends) vs. part time (evenings) vs. full time (daytime) – affect skills development? How does learning in disciplines with long-established online instruction like nursing or public health compare to emerging areas of online instruction like graduate-level science and technology? Can analogies be drawn between the learning styles of so-called digital immigrants (Salazar-Marquez, 2017) and digital natives in online learning environments and the learning styles of international and domestic graduate students in traditional learning environments?

Mentoring in online programs has also been a cause for concern. The topic of graduate-level mentoring was discussed in a previous section but the online environment poses a unique set of challenges, particularly with respect to team-based learning and the mentor–mentee relationship in research training. The concept of "e-mentoring" has been proposed, which includes such techniques as email, telecommunications, discussion boards, blogs, and listserves (Columbaro, 2009), but no studies have looked at its efficacy in comparison to the face-to-face mentoring techniques described earlier. Similar techniques can be used for team-based learning but few studies exist on their effectiveness.

How far does online content mastery take one toward the attainment of independent thought and scholarship? How does the graduate education community balance the democratization of graduate-level education through online instruction with maintaining program quality and improving persistence rates? Unlike some of the other research topics proposed in this monograph, existing comparison groups are waiting for study. For example, how do students with online MBA degrees compare in terms of skills development and career success relative to those with so-called traditional MBAs? Similar comparative studies could be carried out with the EdD. These studies could then be expanded to other degrees and narrowed to evaluate specific content that is delivered through online and asynchronous methods. In all cases, these comparative studies must be rigorous, methodologically sound, and utilize well-established data sets. Online education is rapidly expanding, especially at the master's level, but it is also rapidly changing. The pedagogical benefits and pitfalls of online education must be properly understood for graduate education to evolve without sacrificing scholarly rigor.

In a similar way to online skills development, other long-standing practices in graduate education must be continually re-evaluated for their purpose and impact. Mentoring practices and teaching assistantships are two examples that have already been touched on. Another example – often considered the coin of the realm of graduate education – is the thesis or dissertation.

How Are Theses and Dissertations Changing?

As the graduate education community continues the move from electronic theses and dissertations (ETDs) to purely digital ones[4] (Edminster & Moxley, 2002), mulls over the manifestation of collaborative research on such realities as joint theses from collaborators (Gale et al., 2010), and grapples with the increasing number of requests for thesis embargoes (Truschke, 2015), how does it reassess the meaning of theses and dissertations from pedagogical and practical standpoints? There has been some limited research on this topic published recently from Australian institutions related to the evaluation of transdisciplinary dissertations (Willetts & Mitchell, 2016) and the evolving practice of thesis by publication (Merga et al., 2019). These are emerging topics in the community; broad-based studies and results are scarce. As a result, some of the references here are from the un-indexed and non–peer-reviewed literature. For the sake of simplicity, the term "dissertation" will be used to describe concepts that are common to dissertations and master's theses. The research questions that are specific to each will be discussed separately.

The Council of Graduate Schools co-sponsored a workshop on the future of the dissertation with ProQuest in early 2016, presentations from which are available online (Council of Graduate Schools, 2017). Many of the relevant research questions are nicely enumerated in a summary of the workshop (McCarthy, 2016):

- What is a dissertation? What is its purpose? Who are its audiences and what are their needs?
- What skills are or might be gained as a result of writing a dissertation? What does completing a dissertation demonstrate?
- What formats besides the proto-monograph would support the desired purposes and results of a dissertation? Can nontraditional formats coexist with traditional ones?

4 ETDs are digital analogues of the traditional thesis or dissertation, such as a PDF version that can be retrieved electronically. Purely digital dissertations are those that exist only on the internet and include such emerging formats as blogs, a collection of posts, or even living documents that include replies and comments to the original material.

- How should/could dissertation research be archived, accessed, disseminated? What is the role of the dissertation in the employment marketplace?
- What cultural and disciplinary barriers exist to rethinking the dissertation?

The #alt-academy (Licastro et al., 2016) has also contributed to this topic, especially with respect to alternative formats and digital dissertations. Some of the questions they address are similar and include:

- How have the skills that a student must demonstrate in a dissertation changed over the years?
- Should the skills reflected in the dissertation be different for a student interested in an academic career from one who is not?
- What is the new role of the humanities dissertation as a basis for a monograph?

Clear disciplinary boundaries exist in the application of these questions. For example, the purpose of the dissertation – and the corresponding practical considerations such as format and embargoes – is clearly different in the sciences and engineering from the humanities and social sciences. Especially in the humanities, the dissertation is still often considered a proto-monograph: a precursor to a book or books that not only secures a tenure-track position but can serve as a source of scholarship for future promotions. This view persists despite evidence that the model is unsustainable. One university publisher who presented at the CGS Dissertation Workshop (Britton, 2016) pointed out that about 5,000 humanities PhDs are awarded annually (a number that rose to over 5,600 in the United States in 2015 [NSF Survey of Earned Doctorates/Doctorate Records File, 2017]) yet, at his publishing company (admittedly one of many but also one of the largest), only 60 of 175 new books published each year are in the humanities. Of those, only a few are based on dissertations and even fewer are from newly minted PhDs. In sciences and engineering, the rush to publish new and impactful results comes with its own set of shortcomings, one of which is to de-emphasize the dissertation whole in favor of the sum of its publishable parts. What should be the format of a well-executed dissertation in sciences and engineering? Is a collection of published papers as separate chapters sufficient to demonstrate independent scholarship, or should it (at a minimum) be book-ended by analysis in the form of an introduction and summary? How do dissertation committees and administrators assign "ownership" to co-authored papers that comprise an individual's dissertation?

The issue of intellectual property protection is common to all disciplines and degree levels but for different reasons. In the case of the proto-monograph there is the concern that publishing one's dissertation online will dissuade publishers from accepting portions of the work as a book or monograph. Worse, there are some who believe that publishing a dissertation – especially a creative work – in this digital age provides others an opportunity to plagiarize from it (Brown, 2010). There is little evidence to support either of these claims, yet the concerns persist. There are some descriptive statistical studies on the use of ETDs and their embargoes (Schöpfel & Prost, 2013) but careful studies on the effectiveness (or lack thereof) of dissertation embargoes at combating plagiarism and protecting intellectual property are needed. What are the documented instances of embargoed and unembargoed dissertations being plagiarized, and at what rate? What are the examples of intellectual property being stolen from published dissertations and how much money may have been lost by would-be inventors because of it? Here is an excellent opportunity for teams of researchers from the humanities, economics, educational psychology, history of science, and information science communities to not only generate new knowledge but perform a service to the graduate education community.

With respect to the master's thesis, there is as much conversation about the need for a stand-alone research master's degree (typically the MS or MA) as there is about the requirement of a thesis for that degree. There are certain disciplines for which a master's degree is still considered a terminal degree, such as the MFA in creative writing (Lim, 2003; Ritter, 2001). There are disciplines that rely heavily on the training of master's-level students for research-oriented careers outside the professoriate, such as library science (Powell et al., 2002) and anthropology (Fiske et al., 2010). But nowhere is the purpose of a master's thesis more ambiguous than in the MS degree, especially within the engineering fields (sometimes called an MSE). There is little or no distinction from an employability standpoint between a part-time coursework-based MS in chemical engineering, for example, and a full-time MS plus thesis in the same field. What then is the pedagogical purpose of the MS thesis? It may meet practical considerations, such as a summary of research results for funders, that may not be fulfilled by a journal publication; does a technical report fulfill the same purpose? Here again, there are enough existing programs with thesis and non-thesis options for comparative studies. As master's education continues to evolve to include more professional science and arts degrees, the drawbacks and benefits of the master's thesis must be clearly delineated. Ultimately, the purpose and impact of theses and dissertations on graduate student career preparation must be evaluated. In addition to the research questions outlined above, there are researchable questions on the purpose and structure of dissertations and theses, as well as on their ultimate impact. How do the dissertations of our most celebrated scholars substantively differ from those who transitioned to different careers? How is the citation pattern for theses and dissertations fundamentally different from the books, book chapters, or journal publications that comprise or follow from them?

Whether demonstrated through a culminating work of scholarship such as a dissertation or through course-based learning outcomes, learning at the graduate level is as worthy of investigation as any other level of instruction. The questions are certainly different and in some ways more difficult to pose and answer – requiring the collaboration of researchers with multiple areas of expertise – but the goals in answering them are ultimately the same: to improve student learning and better prepare students for the lives and professional careers that await them. Understanding the complex interplay among cognitive, interpersonal, and intrapersonal skills development in the context of the social setting that is the graduate school experience as preparation for a productive, lifelong career with an advanced degree is the subject of the next chapter.

2 Graduate Student Career Preparation

At the interface of epistemological questions surrounding graduate student learning and the need for continuous graduate program improvement lie questions about what students actually do with their degrees and how a better understanding of those careers can help better prepare current students. More so than the research questions of the other chapters, the questions posed in this chapter inherently require some long-term longitudinal data collection and analysis. In this respect, they are perhaps more ambitious (and difficult) than any of the other items in this research agenda. That fact should not dissuade us from investigating them.

Also in contrast to the other chapters, these research questions are best presented in some roughly chronological – albeit overlapping – order as opposed to randomly, big-to-small, or order of importance. What graduate students do throughout their careers is as much influenced by their experiences prior to graduate school as it is during and after. Life experiences play a large role in many of these research questions. This human element is what makes these investigations into career preparation particularly challenging but ultimately important.

It is counterintuitive, perhaps, that there is more literature on the factors affecting entry into, persistence during, and success in and after graduate school than on the topics of the previous and subsequent chapters on student learning and program improvement, respectively. It may be the result of a "captive audience" effect that makes graduate student survey results some of the (relatively speaking) easiest and most readily available data to collect and analyze. So, many of the existing studies of factors influencing decisions regarding advanced degrees are based on such surveys, often of small numbers of students in one discipline at a single institution. It is worth reiterating at this point what was stated in the introduction: the focus here will be on foundational research in graduate education as reported in the peer-reviewed literature, with an intentional bias toward more recent articles that provide some broad-based insight into the graduate education experience. That means that, in this chapter especially, many existing studies – in particular older ones – may not be directly cited or described. This is not meant to minimize their importance or impact. Summaries of historical studies in newer publications will be cited where available; the resulting theories that have withstood decades of scrutiny and testing will be intertwined with more recent results. The goal is to bring to the fore those research questions that emerged and remain and are worthy of further investigation. Following the chronological approach, the most logical place to start looking for these persistent and new research questions is with the germination of the career choice: when, how, and why one decides to pursue a graduate education.

Why and When Do People Make Educational Decisions about Graduate Degrees?

The decision to pursue a graduate degree is often based – at least in part – on financial considerations, both current and future. Employment opportunities and earning potential are often cited as key determinants in pursuing an advanced degree; however, studies show that this long-standing assumption – while generally true – comes with many caveats. For example, one study utilizing US census data found that, over their careers, women with PhDs earn only as much as males with a bachelor's degree (Carnevale et al., 2011). A study from the Netherlands showed that the average annual return for a PhD over a master's degree is effectively zero over the first 20 years from attainment (Wouterse et al., 2017). An analysis of data from the US 2013 National Survey of College Graduates (Okahana & Hao, 2019) shows that the earning potential of STEM master's degree holders is strongly influenced by individual characteristics such as race, ethnicity, and gender rather than degree level or disciplinary field alone.

Another key factor is student debt incurred during undergraduate education and anticipated during graduate school; socioeconomic status plays a large role in determining the level of tolerance for acquiring additional debt after obtaining a baccalaureate degree (Belasco et al., 2014; Malcom & Dowd, 2012). The decision to pursue an advanced degree is not an all-or-nothing proposition, however. Some students delay entry into a graduate program to a later date. Roughly half of students entering US graduate schools do so directly after obtaining their baccalaureate degrees (figure 8). These preliminary results suggest that

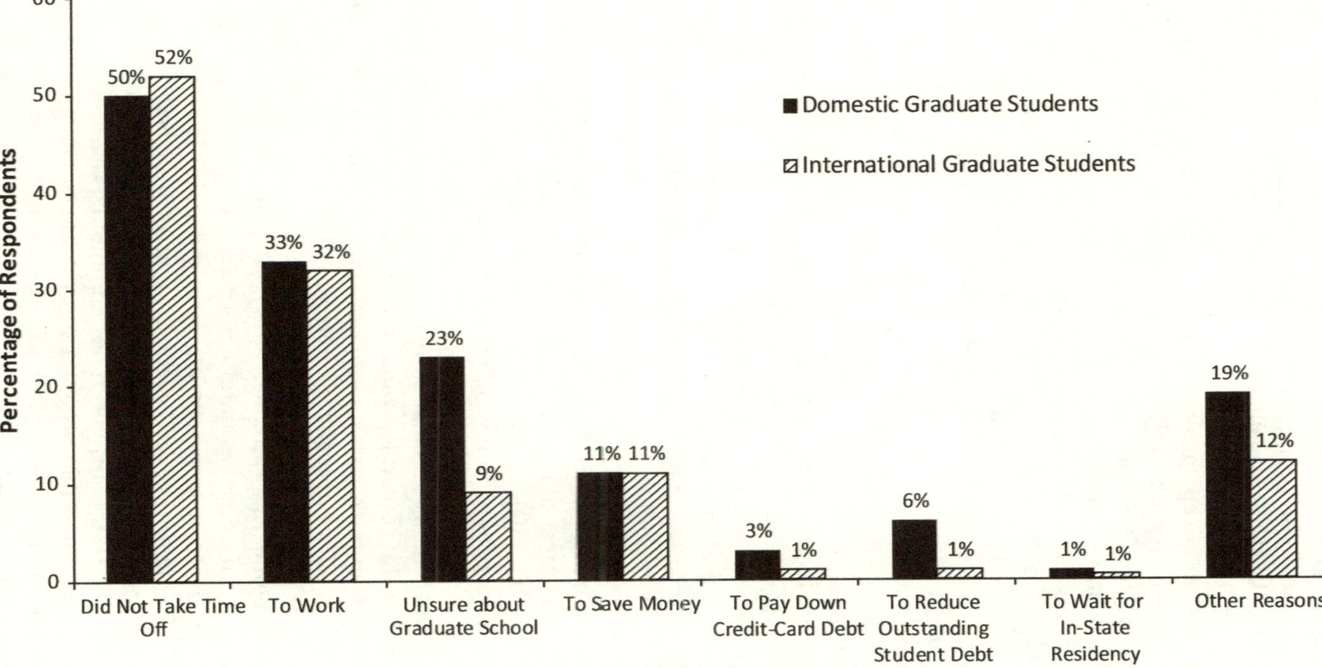

Figure 8. Factors affecting a student's decision to delay entry to graduate school. Source: Unpublished data courtesy Council of Graduate Schools from their 2014 CGS Financial Standing Survey.

undergraduate student debt is not currently a major factor in delaying entrance to a graduate program; however, previous studies found that it could be (Weiler, 1994), especially for master's students (Millett, 2003) and women (Fox, 1992).

There are non-financial factors, as well, for considering graduate school. It is known, for example, that undergraduate research experiences increase the likelihood of participation in graduate research (Lopatto, 2007) and graduate degree completion (Bauer & Bennett, 2003). Socioeconomic factors such as parental educational level (Mullen et al., 2003; Perna, 2004; Walpole, 2008) and (perhaps related) attending an elite, private undergraduate institution increase the likelihood of attending graduate school (Eide et al., 1998). For underrepresented minorities, faculty support through undergraduate research experiences and informal actives can mitigate socioeconomic factors (Deangelo, 2016). The influences of family and personal considerations on the decision-making process are still poorly understood, not only for URM students but international students. Those are the subjects of later specific research questions. For now, this research question focuses on broad, personal characteristics that influence one's motivation to pursue an advanced degree. Results from these studies could better inform the programmatic-based research questions that follow in this chapter concerning funding models, retention, and time to degree.

One recent survey (Guerin et al., 2015) of over 400 graduate students in a variety of disciplines at an Australian research university found that there are five broad areas of motivation for students undertaking "higher degrees by research" (HDRs): encouragement by family and/or friends, intrinsic motivation (desire to invent/create/discover new things), (undergraduate) lecturer influence, desire for research experience, and career enhancement/change. Similar studies – with similar results – have been conducted in the United Kingdom (Wellington & Sikes, 2006) and the United States (Jablonski, 2001) in the area of motivation for the EdD. Investigators in several countries have also reported on student motivation to undertake PhD careers in certain disciplines such as history (Brailsford, 2010) and engineering (Mokhtar, 2012). What are the influences of such geographical differences as cultural norms and employment market demands on the decision to pursue a graduate degree? How do these decisions differ by gender? A recent study explored the reasons women enter physics doctoral programs at a higher rate than chemistry doctoral programs (Dabney & Tai, 2014) and reported that first-year undergraduate classroom experiences had a significant influence. The authors further recommended that future studies not only compare women to men within a discipline but compare men and women across disciplinary fields

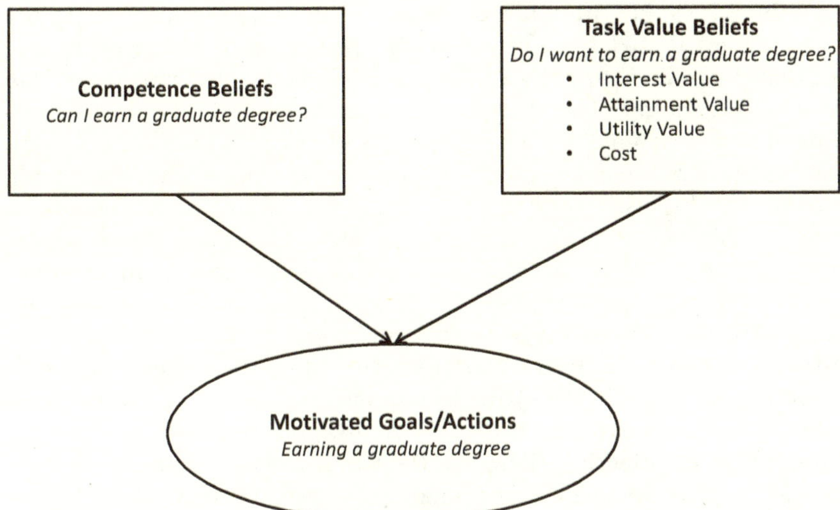

Figure 9. Simplified expectancy-value theory model for the action of pursuing a graduate degree. Adapted from Eccles, 2005.

to better understand motivation and influences. One longitudinal study from investigators at Vanderbilt University (K. Robertson et al., 2010) showed that individual differences in general cognitive ability lead to differences in educational, occupational, and creative outcomes decades later but that educational-vocational interests and lifestyle preferences also play key roles in predicting future career outcomes. This "science of talent development" approach implies that early interventions that aim to influence career choice and persistence in graduate school can be effective, especially for students from underrepresented groups.

The application of motivation theory has been used at the undergraduate level to investigate factors affecting career choice. For example, expectancy-value theory (Eccles, 2005) was used to study student motivation to choose engineering as a career (Matusovich et al., 2010). The primary influence on an undergraduate engineering career choice was a student's sense of self – also known as attainment value – as opposed to pure interest in the field. One value category alone was insufficient to explain persistence in the undergraduate engineering career, however. In an adaptation of this theory to pursuing a graduate degree (figure 9), the choice to engage in an activity is dictated by input from two primary sets of personal beliefs: competency and values. Is expectancy-value theory a sufficient model to explain interest in pursuing a graduate degree?

Are the values that influence decisions on an undergraduate major the same values that determine interest in pursuing an advanced degree in that same field, or even a different field? Here, the concept of "life course" may help differentiate between decisions made at different periods of a student's life and may help track changes in motivation toward pursuing an advanced degree at various career stages. The direct pathway model (high school to undergraduate degree to graduate school) is implicit in many of these studies. This model is changing; it is even inappropriate in some graduate-level disciplines such as education, business, and health care (Snyder et al., 2016) where part-time enrollments are large. The decision to return to graduate school for working adults comprises a different set of considerations, including work stress and family support (Kirby et al., 2004). Expectancy-value theory has also been applied, for example, to investigate the motivations of returning graduate students in engineering (Peters & Daly, 2013). Some of these life-stage research questions are treated separately from the motivational questions in the ensuing sections, though they could easily be studied alongside one another.

An emerging theoretical construct for studying graduate school intentions is Social Cognitive Career Theory (SCCT). SCCT brings together conceptually related constructs such as self-efficacy and expectancy-value theory and uses them to analyze more common career outcomes such as satisfaction and employment stability rather than solely discipline-specific metrics such as salary (Lent et al., 2002). (We will see in a subsequent research question that career outcomes play an important role in emerging career success models.) A recent article described the application of SCCT to study over 1,000 US undergraduate STEM students' intentions to attend graduate school. They found that self-efficacy had the strongest effect on intent to pursue a graduate degree. Outcomes expectations was also a strong correlator but only for those pursuing the PhD; it did not correlate with those intending to pursue a master's degree. Although this particular result could be related to the emphasis placed on the PhD as a research degree in the STEM disciplines, it points to the need to differentiate between degree levels when conducting research on graduate education. Similarly, this study highlighted the differences between African American and Hispanic students in their intent to pursue a PhD, arguing for further disaggregation of the URM designation when investigating factors influencing career decisions. Undergraduate institution type can also play a role in SCCT. Deangelo (2008, 2010) found that institutional selectivity positively correlates with aspirations to the PhD for white students but that students of color are more influenced by faculty encouragement.

When deciding to pursue a graduate degree, as important as intrinsic and extrinsic forces is the availability of accurate information, especially at critical decision-making stages. Here studies are even more limited and their results are not available to prospective students in any systematic way. What is the return on investment for obtaining an advanced degree? What are the measurable benefits of a direct pathway to an advanced degree vs. returning as an adult learner? Some data are available for US institutions through the National Center for Education Statistics (NCES) and National Center for Science and Engineering Statistics (NCSES) and, to some extent, from individual programs themselves; however, the ability to objectively compare institutions and programs is missing at the graduate level.

Research on the student decision-making process will have immediate impact. The lack of objective, timely, meaningful data on graduate programs and their outcomes has clear implications. It is no wonder that rankings are a significant source of information for students and a measure of program quality. Unfortunately, rankings create a system whereby the evaluating body – whether a national organization of well-meaning scholars or a national media publication whose primary aim is to increase profits – sets the rules; programs reflexively respond to them. The faculty and administrator conversations then devolve into ones about ranking methodology rather than true program improvement, and student decisions are based upon what is important to the ranking agencies rather than what is important to themselves. There is no evidentiary research suggesting that the metrics these rankings use are the correct ones. There is, however, evidence that the metrics are easily manipulated (Ghiasi et al., 2019). Even a preliminary study on the impact of ranking metrics on student enrollment (from a holistic point of view) would be welcome.

These are tragic ironies: lack of accurate and timely career information for prospective students living in the Information Age; lack of career data and an appropriate platform for their dissemination from those of us whose livelihood it is to generate new knowledge. Despite these flaws, good graduate degree programs exist and exceptional students continue to flock to them. It is just not clear why. Nor do we have adequate information on how students make life decisions after entering graduate school. That is the topic of the next step in the educational process.

What Factors Influence Career Decisions While in Graduate School?

Aside from their initial intentions in seeking an advanced degree and the didactic training and mentoring they receive while in graduate school, how do graduate students make career decisions while in graduate

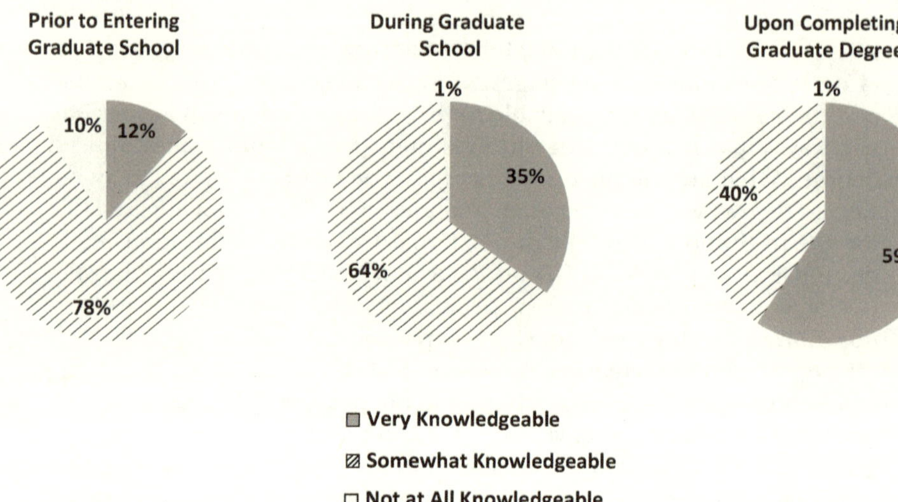

Figure 10. Graduate school deans' opinions on extent of graduate student knowledge on career opportunities in research degree programs. With corrected data from Wendler et al., 2012.

school? The self-efficacy and expectancy-value theory models of the previous sections certainly apply here, as do the influences of various mentoring activities described in chapter 1, but just like baccalaureate students, post-baccalaureate students may not consider the next step in their careers until they are much closer to degree completion. Nevertheless, information is continuously being made available to them and they have some ideas about their career plans even if those ideas are difficult to formalize. How do graduate students' career aspirations evolve while they are in graduate school?

An online survey from the Council of Graduate Schools of 213 graduate deans at US and Canadian institutions (Wendler et al., 2012) showed that graduate deans believe that the majority of students in graduate programs are somewhat knowledgeable or very knowledgeable about career options prior to entering graduate school and that their knowledge of career options generally increases as they progress through graduate school (figure 10). Still – by the deans' estimations – a full 40% of students remain only "somewhat knowledgeable" about their career options upon degree completion. Aside from the fact that this is an opinion survey only, what studies like this cannot show is whether prospective students who opted not to complete their degrees or who opted for careers well outside of their disciplinary training received the critical information they needed to reach that decision and whether the information was accurate. Comprehensive, direct surveying of students before, during, and after the career decision point is required, as well as longitudinal studies that measure the outcomes of those decisions. Studies of this kind are starting to emerge.

Investigators at the Georgia Institute of Technology have studied how student attitudes regarding academic research and teaching careers evolve during graduate school. In one study, survey results from 400 science and engineering PhD students showed that those with a stronger "taste for science" were more inclined to pursue academic research careers than industrial careers (Roach & Sauermann, 2010). A more recent study from these same investigators showed that PhD students in life sciences, chemistry, and physics all exhibited a decrease in interest for academic careers (both teaching and research) from early to late stages in their graduate education experiences, although interest in both remained high compared to interest in government and start-up company jobs (Sauermann & Roach, 2012). Most importantly perhaps, this study reinforces the fact that there is an oversupply of PhD graduates interested in faculty careers relative to the number of available positions (Roach & Sauermann, 2017). Further studies are needed in a wider array of disciplines from a more diverse institutional pool to make career-choice research more robust. How can (or should) predictions of workforce needs that are often used to justify federal investment in graduate education be used in career advising? Are such workforce projections even useful in shaping student's decisions? Little follow-up has been done on workforce projections. A recent report from the US National Academies highlighted the difficulties with such workforce projections, including the non-linear career pathways of degree holders; that is, those with a STEM degree do not always work in STEM-related fields, nor are all STEM-related jobs held by those with STEM degrees. More economists, statisticians, and informaticists are needed on research projects related to disciplinary workforce definitions, real-time workforce analytics, and skills application in order to provide accurate and timely information to prospective students during key decision-making periods of their careers.

The issue of attrition is addressed in more detail in chapter 3 from the standpoint of program improvement. Certainly personal factors are involved in attrition and retention, especially when students voluntarily exit a graduate program prior to completion as opposed to those who do not complete because of academic or research performance. The factors affecting decisions to continue, cease, or suspend pursuit of an advanced degree are as many and varied as those affecting the choice of which type of career to pursue upon completion, although there is undoubtedly overlap. Family formation is an example of one such factor that is beginning to emerge in the literature as an influencer of career choice. Decisions surrounding anticipated family formation differentially affect women and men, a fact reflected in the focus of the emerging literature (Allison & Ralston, 2018; Craig et al., 2018; Mirick & Wladkowski, 2018). (The specifics of factors affecting women's graduate school experiences are deferred to a subsequent research question on program improvement and underrepresented groups.) However, common issues influence the graduate school career choices of graduate students planning for families. A recent study in the graduate medical education arena (Vassallo et al., 2019) describes the challenges of applying federal guidelines such as the Family and Medical Leave Act (FMLA) to trainees on stipends and fellowships for birth and non-birth parents. Mental health (also discussed in chapter 3) is another factor that can be viewed from both the programmatic and personal levels and requires effective policy and best practices to reach the largest number of people it affects. How do federal, state, and local polices affect the career decision process, especially when superimposed upon evolving societal mores and cultural changes? Unlike other research areas, is longitudinal or historical information even relevant for making decisions in a "just-in-time" world? Regardless of the factor, accurate and timely information is essential for making well-informed career choices. The sources of that information are varied but increasingly come from centralized institutional resources such as graduate schools and career centers.

The career advising community – with its traditional undergraduate focus – has some information on the evolving career-choice needs of graduate students. Whether centralized within a graduate school or decentralized by discipline (such as business or law), career offices generally provide three types of services to graduate students (that are similar to those for undergraduates): career counseling and advising, programming, and placement services (Lehker & Furlong, 2006). Unlike undergraduate placement services, however, career offices can serve as a neutral place for graduate students to discuss their career options away from the influence of their research advisors. Programming typically takes the form of workshops, the topics of which range from résumé writing to interview preparation. A recent study of 788 graduate students at a research-intensive US university (Rizzolo et al., 2016) found that the majority of students desired field-specific career-development training. Is adequate career-opportunity information made available to graduate students prior to these later-stage job-placement training sessions and is it specific enough by discipline to meet their needs? A 2001 report (Golde & Dore, 2001) indicated that less than half of doctoral students surveyed said that workshops on conducting a job search outside of academia were available. That number has undoubtedly increased in the intervening years; however, what aspects of job searches are most effective and how do they affect graduate student career choices? What are the effects of such broad factors as the economy and geopolitical conflict on not only job opportunities but career choice? How can the career advising community effectively access and utilize what is often disciplinary-based career information? Graduate schools and career advising centers can team on research projects to provide university-specific data but larger efforts involving collaborations among professional advising associations, associations of graduate schools, and relevant disciplinary professional societies are needed to determine the short- and long-term impacts of career information availability, employment, and career decisions on career success. One such area of collaboration is growing and requires its own set of investigations: professional development training.

What Are the Long-Term Impacts of Structured Professional Development Activities during Graduate School on Career Success?

As a subset of the career success and career development research questions previously posed, one growing area in need of assessment is that of professional development activities while in graduate school. This topic is posed as a separate category of questions simply because of the emphasis it is receiving; however, all possible current and future professional development needs is too broad a subject for consideration here. Graduate schools increasingly invest money, time, and human capital in offering professional development activities for graduate students in all disciplines. The set of skills comprising professional development were discussed in chapter 1. In this section, the career impact of professional development activities is the focus. What are the correct professional skills to develop and how are they best delivered? What is the impact on other disciplinary skills of the time commitment necessary to develop professional development skills?

Professional development offerings include activities (workshops, seminars, direct funding, and structured activities) in such areas as effective communication, project planning and management, international experiences, and public service and outreach. These activities have been developed partly in response to specific employer requests and partly to better prepare students for the multiple career pathways they will likely face. Typically, some kind of evaluation is performed at the end of the workshop or activity but the assessment tends to end there. What the community really needs to know is whether and how these activities better prepare graduate students for successful careers, both in the short term (employability) and the long term (career success).

The Council of Graduate Schools issued a report on professional development activities in STEM graduate education (Denecke et al., 2017). Their report was based on 857 surveys from deans, directors of graduate study, and professional development program directors at 226 US and Canadian institutions of higher education. They found that most existing professional development programs combine centralized and program-specific activities focusing on the development of skills that are considered transferable across multiple careers and disciplines. These skills include communication, mentoring, and leadership across all disciplines and, in the STEM disciplines, research ethics, research development, technology commercialization, and entrepreneurship. There are currently no universally accepted curricula for the development and assessment of these skills but there are emerging frameworks and needs assessments that help identify what activities are necessary. For example, the biochemistry PhD program at the University of Toronto offers a professional development course that addresses such topics as mentorship and research ethics (N. Lee & Reithmeier, 2013). Less is known about the impact of these activities. Institutions assess the effectiveness of these professional development programs in various ways, including participant and employer surveys and career tracking, but no systematic studies have been performed to date on the impact of these professional development activities on career success.

The impact of professional development activities on other aspects of the graduate student experience is also mostly unknown. For example, do these activities significantly lengthen time to degree as some advisors would argue? Does participation in professional skill-building activities adversely impact the research productivity of graduate students? The National Research Council has developed a set of report briefs (National Research Council, 2014b; Pellegrino & Hilton, 2013) on what they term "21st-century competencies." Similarly, the US National Academies of Sciences, Engineering, and Medicine's most recent report on graduate STEM education (National Academies of Sciences, Engineering, and Medicine, 2018) lists what they term "core educational elements" for master's and PhD degrees that include the development of leadership, communication, and professional development skills, as well as reports on the assessment of inter- and intrapersonal skills development at the undergraduate level (National Academies of Sciences, Engineering, and Medicine, 2017a). These are intra- and interpersonal transferable skills that are categorized separately from cognitive skills yet constitute a growing set of skills that lead not only to deeper learning but purportedly to more desirable workplace outcomes. Although focused almost exclusively on K–12 and undergraduate educational experiences, the current research has implications for graduate education. As understanding of intra- and interpersonal skills development improves at the undergraduate level, what does this mean for the level or even necessity of professional development skills programs at the graduate level?

What research there is on the development of professional development skills at the graduate level is narrowly focused on such topics as entrepreneurship (Hayter et al., 2017), written communication skills (Tarabochia & Madden, 2018), science policy (Bernstein et al., 2017), global competence (Mitchell, 2019; Mitchell et al., 2016; Slantcheva-Durst & Danowski, 2018), and even research competence in the so-called non-research professional graduate degrees (Weaver et al., 2017). It should also be obvious to the reader at this point that much of this work is limited to the STEM fields. Are the professional development skills required by master's-level artists and architects the same as those required by PhD-level molecular biologists? How does the emergence of interdisciplinary teams affect not only which skills require further development but who is responsible for providing that training? Does the development of professional skills in graduate school properly set the stage for further skills development as one's career develops?

Professional skills should persist after graduation and into the workplace. Advanced degree holders are trained to adapt to changing research methods and techniques, teach themselves new tools, and learn from the literature and professional communities in which they work. Why, then, do graduate degree holders continue to accumulate student debt to develop a new skill in a few weeks, such as through stackable courses in coding boot camps (Chea, 2013)? One unpublished study from the University of Pennsylvania (Christensen et al., 2013) found that of all the students enrolled in at least one lecture of their 32 courses in a variety of fields available online through Coursera – nearly two-thirds of whom were from outside the United States – 44% self-reported having previously attained education beyond a bachelor's degree. MOOCs are, of course, not the only (or even most preferable) mode for lifelong learning in all skill areas but they do provide opportunities for enhancing specific post-graduate skills.

Preparation for lifelong learning is often considered a component of baccalaureate degree programs but there is much to be learned about how graduate degree holders continue to learn as their careers – and technology – develop. Little is known about the careers students pursue, much less how their graduate degrees prepared them for those careers and its transitions. How many master's and PhD holders outside of the education disciplines transition at some point to primary and secondary teaching careers? Is the certification process easier or more difficult for them? Are they fundamentally better teachers? Do dual-degree holders such as JD-PhD or MD-PhD enjoy more successful careers than those with individual advanced degrees? How do advanced degrees prepare students to transition into business opportunities, start-up companies, and executive positions? What aspects of advanced-degree training are most important for success in any career? Of all the professional skills and competence described in this section, one might argue that ethical conduct is simultaneously the most overlooked yet most important professional skill learned in graduate school. This topic requires the following separate discussion.

How Do Graduate Students Develop Ethical Conduct Expertise That Will Stay with Them Their Entire Professional Careers, Regardless of Career Choice?

More than just a learned skill, ethical conduct is a lens through which most activities – including professional and personal – can be viewed. The focus of this research question is on professional responsibility, of course, but the key questions really are about how ethical conduct can be inculcated in graduate students such that it persists through career transitions and societal evolutions. So important is this issue that it deserves separate investigation from other professional development skills. Management, leadership, and communication skills may need to be adapted as one transitions from job to job. Ethical responsibility, however, must persist.

Federal guidelines (National Institutes of Health, 2009) requiring training in ethics and the responsible conduct of research (here treated singly for convenience but certainly worthy of separate investigation) – while well-intentioned – have relegated these topics to perfunctory online training that is typically delivered asynchronously and online (Collaborative Institutional Training Initiative at the University of Miami, 2016). No broad-based studies have yet been performed on their effectiveness but one survey-based study of 48 graduate students found that, although short-term ethics training increased knowledge of responsible conduct of research, it did not alter moral judgment (Schmaling & Blume, 2009). By one measure, ethics training has been ineffective to date in mitigating research misconduct – the number of cases acted upon by the US Department of Health and Human Services Office of Research Integrity (ORI) continues to grow (US Department of Health and Human Services, The Office of Research Integrity, 2015). The transparency with which these cases are reported on and investigated is also increasing. The American Association for the Advancement of Science

(AAAS), for example, publishes a quarterly report on professional ethics in the scientific community (American Association for the Advancement of Science, 2016). Although these statistics are limited and one could argue that the ethics training has actually heightened awareness of reporting research misconduct, the fact remains that little is known about the reasons for research misconduct and what lasting effects ethical training may have on advanced degree–holders' careers.

The teaching and learning of ethics and the responsible conduct of research (RCR) may be viewed in the context of the development of research skills or alongside other professional skills such as effective communication and project management. There have been disciplinary-based efforts to incorporate ethics and responsible conduct of research training directly into the graduate curriculum, for example through "microinsertion" into graduate-level engineering courses (M. Davis & Feinerman, 2012); however, one survey of 88 US universities with graduate degree programs in statistics or biostatics found that only about one-third of them required an ethics course (L. Lee et al., 2015). Another study utilizing a bottom-up approach to incorporate ethical training into research environments (Hildt et al., 2019) found that requiring STEM graduate students to apply published professional ethical codes to the development of context-specific guidelines for the laboratory research environment (as opposed to the field for which they are normally developed) was effective. This approach is based upon previously published literature suggesting that ethics training should occur in an institutional context comprising both organizational context and the peer environment (National Academies of Sciences, Engineering, and Medicine, 2017b). The involvement of all research-environment collaborators – including faculty – in the development of context-specific ethics guidelines is important since the ethical conduct of faculty advisors and mentors is of concern to graduate students, especially with respect to plagiarism and authorship (Becker, 2019). Rubrics for the design and evaluation of curriculum-based RCR training have been developed (Tractenberg & FitzGerald, 2012) that articulate the desired skills, demonstrate their development from novice to proficient levels, and provide a framework for skills assessment over the scientist's career. Complicating the development and assessment of ethical skills for scholars are cultural variations in values and mores. Even within narrowly defined fields such as bioethics, it has taken the involvement of intergovernmental agencies to link datasets and increase cooperation in ethics training and information dissemination (ten Have & Ang, 2007; UNESCO, 2007) from various countries.

There is some literature on ethics training in non-science disciplines such as business management (Small, 2006) and public administration

(Menzel, 1997). The epistemology of ethics certainly underpins several of the humanities and social sciences disciplines. There are also ethical concerns about the use of private funding to support graduate students in the social sciences, arts, and humanities where graduate students may feel pressure to represent the position of a funder of their fellowship, for example, in a positive light (Stein et al., 2019). But there is little in the way of formal training – much less research – on ethical training in many non-science disciplines. There is even pushback on ethics reviews of research in the social sciences (Schrag, 2011).

This research topic is a rich one. How does the need for ethics and RCR training vary by discipline? What training methods are most effective? What are the influences of funding-agency requirements on this type of training and are sufficient funds supplied to meet mandates? What effects do perceptions of institutional review board effectiveness have on the ability to train graduate students on the ethical conduct of research? Why are sources of private funding for graduate students viewed differently in the social sciences and humanities than in the science and engineering fields and are those views justified? How do programs adequately certify that their graduates will conduct their future scholarship ethically and responsibly? What are the legal ramifications if they fail to provide this training? Since little is known about the careers of advanced degree holders, it follows that little is known about how ethics and RCR training are retained and applied throughout one's career.

The topic of ethical training leads naturally to the next topic because the expectation is that ethical training will stay with students as they transition to the workplace. The transition itself can pose ethical challenges. For example, how do political science advanced degree holders determine which nonprofit think tanks best suit not only their research training but their personal political ideals? How do pharmaceutical scientists trained in rigorous research methods transition to the commercial enterprise where profits can clash with professional ethics? These topics and more are the basis for the next research question on transitioning to the workplace.

How Do Graduate Students Effectively Transition from Study to Work?

The transition from graduate school to the workforce comprises a complex, interrelated set of personal and professional changes that can be as monumental as any other defining moment in a person's life. This transition could certainly be studied from a social-psychology standpoint in the same way that other life-changing events such as childbirth, retirement, or career change are investigated; however, a focus on the transferable skills discussed in chapter 1 on the school–work transition would

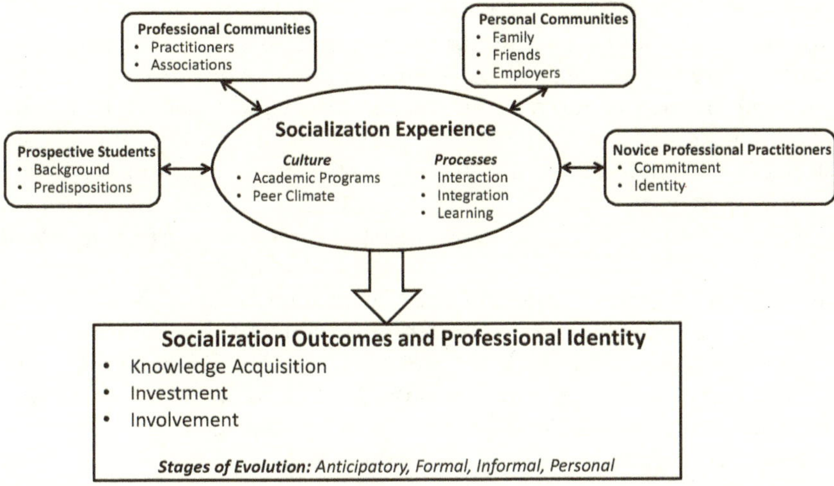

Figure 11. Socialization model for graduate students. Adapted from Weidman et al., 2001.

be of most immediate utility. The transferable skills discussion was, of course, predicated on a clear definition of what those skills should be; research on the transition to the workforce would require similarly specific information on what former students do in their current jobs. Neither of those components of the transition is well understood but, taken as a whole, the study-to-work or school-to-workforce transition is worthy of some model-based investigation.

We have already seen that socialization theory has been broadly applied to the career preparation of graduate and professional students (Weidman et al., 2001). It is worth revisiting this theory as it applies to the transition to the workforce. In this model (figure 11), socialization in graduate school comprises university climate factors such as academic program, interaction and integration with peers and faculty, and of course learning. It evolves over time from the anticipatory stage prior to entry through to the personal stage as a practitioner; it results in the core outcomes of socialization: knowledge acquisition, investment, and involvement. Investment and involvement are heavily influenced by advisors and mentors (see the discussion in chapter 1), especially in research degrees. The role of advisors in the development of future faculty has been separately researched from this socialization-theory point of view (Austin, 2002; Austin et al., 2009; Weidman & Stein, 2003). In general, these studies find that graduate students do not receive systematic opportunities to develop the necessary skills for faculty careers. How well does socialization theory describe preparation for all degree-compatible careers? Are the predictions these models imply realized? For example, socialization theory models the socialization experience and the outcomes of knowledge acquisition, professional investment, and professional involvement as being influenced by various communities in the socialization experience. The implication, then, is that those who do not attain the necessary knowledge or possess the necessary professional investment or involvement were somehow disconnected or negatively influenced by one or more of these communities. Is this prediction borne out by data? Do non-completing students fit this model as well? These complementary research questions have enormous implications for the success of students from nontraditional backgrounds and those from underrepresented groups. How can deficiencies in factors such as personal communities be positively influenced?

The potential research topics on student socialization theory range from these general questions to the more specific. For example, internships and externships are now a component of graduate programs where they previously did not exist. How do training practices such as industrial internships fit into and influence the socialization-theory model? A study on university–industry graduate training collaborations comes from Norway (Thune, 2009). As in other European countries (Wallgren & Dahlgren, 2007) and Australia (Harman, 2004), university–industry collaborations in doctoral training are increasingly common. As illustrated in figure 12, Thune has reviewed the current research on these university–industry doctoral degrees and classified the studies according to the factors they investigated in the collaboration. Key findings suggest that selected outcomes, such as self-assessment of the experience, career ambitions, and numbers of publications, are not very different from non-collaborative control groups; however, the likelihood of private-sector employment increases. This study is itself a research agenda and proposes several sound hypotheses (or propositions), including two complementary propositions related to the career trajectories of participants:

> Collaborating with firms during the doctoral degree influences career trajectories (sector of employment) and increases the likelihood of private sector employment.
>
> Differences in career trajectories (sector of employment) is [*sic*] explainable by individual characteristics (age, gender, family background, prior employment) and not by collaborative experience during the doctoral degree. (Thune, 2009)

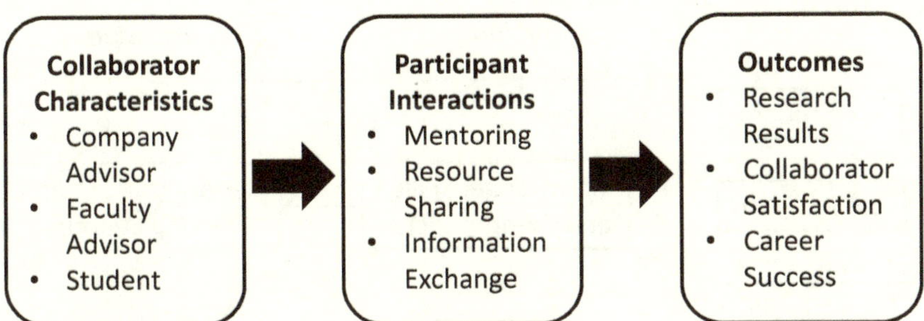

Figure 12. Relationship between factors in the study of university–industry doctoral programs. Adapted from Thune, 2009.

The author points to the need for longitudinal research on not only career trajectories but the research products of the university–industry collaboration in order to effectively test these propositions.

As the study from Norway illustrates, much of the available information and research comes from the sciences and engineering communities. Recent reports on the STEM workforce (National Academies of Sciences, Engineering and Medicine, 2016; National Science Board, 2015; Sargent, 2014) have painted a complex picture of how the professional STEM workforce is constituted, including the heterogeneity in workforce preparation described earlier. Not only is there an opportunity to study the effects of diversity and inclusion on certain sectors of the workforce but there is a need to investigate the influences of different communities on the effectiveness of an inclusive workforce. For example, advanced degree holders from historically Black colleges and universities (HBCUs) may combine with those from predominantly white institutions (PWI) to form a racially diverse workforce; however, is their respective workforce preparation the same as that from more inclusive institutions? How do their school-to-work transitions compare? Other more discipline-based reports show the impact of such factors as federal funding on the workforce in heavily academic research-dominated disciplines like the biomedical sciences (National Institutes of Health, 2012; Pickett et al., 2015). A recent workshop report identified broad factors influencing the so-called pipeline progress from doctoral degree to first job in the area of psychology (Kaslow, Bangasser, Grus, McCutcheon, & Fowler, 2018). Transitional influences include trainee factors (accomplishments, personality and interpersonal factors, goodness of fit), trainer factors (professional competence, investment in trainee's development), program factors (status and nature, infrastructure), and systemic factors (inclusivity, bottlenecks,

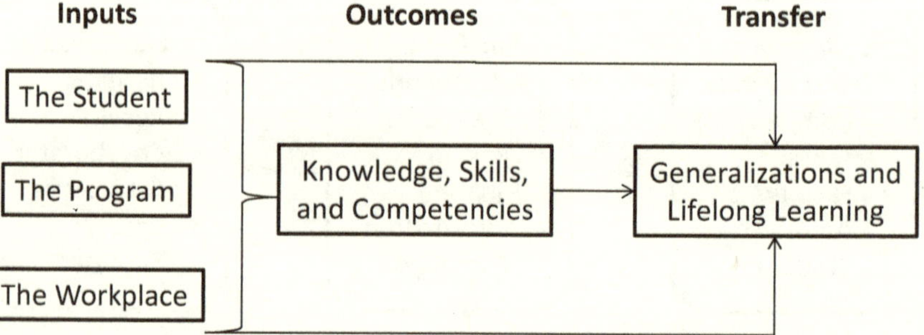

Figure 13. A transfer process model for graduate-level training. Adapted from Baldwin & Ford, 1988.

financial support, and pipeline preparation). More broadly, recent survey results from the Council of Graduate Schools show that workplace transitions are fluid and that movement between sectors, such as between the private sector and academia, are not as unidirectional as the pipeline model suggests (Okahana, 2018, 2019).

Aside from these studies on specific segments of the workforce as they currently exist, little research has been conducted on the best ways to influence their constitution, especially for those from underrepresented groups and nontraditional backgrounds. Even less is known about the transition from graduate school to the permanent workforce, especially in non-STEM areas such as the humanities and fine arts, although underemployment and careers as contingent faculty have certainly been a topic of much recent discussion (American Academy of Arts and Sciences, 2015). Can the professoriate workforce be adequately modeled so that the impact of reducing the number of contingent faculty can be measured before such changes are enacted? Employability is a practical yet ever-present concern in the graduate education community. Here again, existing research on life transitions such as from secondary to postsecondary education and from the baccalaureate to the workplace should serve as the basis for these studies. The organizational-behavior field provides several models with which to work (see, for example, the NRC report "Education for Life and Work" [Pellegrino & Hilton, 2013] for an overview at the K–16 levels), including one (Baldwin & Ford, 1988) that categorizes the conditions under which training transfers to the workplace. If one adapts this model to the graduate school as workplace (figure 13), student characteristics might include some of the factors described in previous sections such as cognitive ability and motivation; program characteristics might include research and didactic training. Workplace factors would comprise supervisor and peer support as well as opportunities to utilize knowledge, skills, and competence. Is this model as appropriate for research-based skills and independent scholars as it is for vocational skills and continuing education? If so, does it apply equally well to academic and private-sector careers? Does the model appropriately account for differences in scholastic preparation, cultural norms, and career aspirations? An understanding of these transfer models must be used to assist students in finding meaningful careers, especially outside of the academy and especially for those from underrepresented groups. Such transfer models must also be used to study a common career transition for doctoral degree holders: the postdoctoral appointment.

What Is the Role of Postdoctoral Training in the Career Development of an Advanced Degree Holder?

Research on the influences and benefits of postdoctoral training is a monograph topic unto itself, so only a preliminary attempt to bound it is given here. It is of such importance to some disciplines (such as the biomedical sciences) and obscurity to others (such as most humanities) that research findings with broad-based impact are unlikely. Nevertheless, the perceived relevance of postdoctoral training is so influential to the graduate school experience in some disciplines that specific studies demand immediate attention.

Even basic statistics on postdoctoral scholars (postdocs) are hard to come by. It is estimated that there are some 250,000–400,000 postdoctoral scholars worldwide (National Academies, 2014). The National Postdoctoral Association estimates that there are roughly 79,000 postdocs in the United States (Ferguson et al., 2014). In the science, engineering, and health sciences fields, the 2015 Survey of Graduate Students and Postdoctorates in Science and Engineering co-sponsored by NSF and NIH showed that the number of postdocs in US academic institutions was around 64,000 despite recent declines in the number of postdocs in the biological sciences and clinical medicine (Arbeit & Kang, 2017). Even more so than with graduate students, little tracking of postdocs is done outside of institutional settings; even less is known about why graduate students transition to postdoctoral positions and when they make those decisions. Despite attempts at working definitions of a postdoctoral experience by the National Postdoctoral Association, for example, there are few formal structures for postdoctoral training at the national and international levels, so funding can come from a variety of sources and the appointment can be with research venues outside of the academy, including industry, government facilities, and nongovernmental agencies. Moreover, the source of funding may be de-linked from the location of the actual postdoctoral training.

We do know that postdoctoral training can be important to an academic career but what about the myriad of compatible career options that doctoral candidates face? A recent survey of nearly 6,000 PhD students at 39 US research universities found that 78% of respondents in the biological and life sciences and 42% in other science and engineering fields believed that at least one year of postdoctoral training was required for a career in industry (Sauermann & Roach, 2016). It also found that challenging labor markets tend to increase the number of graduate students who pursue postdoctoral education. As well, the study highlights the need for better career counseling for graduate students.

One aspect of postdoctoral training that can impact decisions made in graduate school and beyond is that of an international experience. International research experiences contribute to the development of so-called global competence, which is valued by employers in advanced degree holders (Denecke et al., 2017; Grindel, 2006; Mitchell et al., 2016). International research training groups (IRTGs) provide opportunities to students and trainees at various educational stages, including the postdoctoral level. More common at the postdoctoral level, however, are individual international experiences. The numbers of postdoctoral researchers involved in these experiences are difficult to track and evaluate. Some information is available from funding agencies. A review of the now-defunct NSF International Research Fellowship Program (IRFP) (Martinez et al., 2012) supports what is generally known from the IRTG research; namely, that funded fellows had a larger number and percentage of publications with foreign co-authors than non-funded applicants without sacrificing overall research productivity or professional achievement. This study did not evaluate the development of specific skills or competence, however, and was limited to the disciplines and participating countries supported by NSF. The questions that they posed provide opportunities for further research. How does the extent to which postdocs and graduate students participate in international collaborations affect skills development and employability relative to those who do not? How does the availability of international experiences at the postdoctoral level affect decisions to delay these experiences in graduate school? What are the relative benefits of an international postdoctoral experience relative to a domestic one? What are the effects of socioeconomic status, URM status, and familial obligations on the likelihood of undertaking a postdoctoral appointment and subsequent career success if one is not taken?

The negative impacts of prolonged postdoctoral experiences in the biomedical sciences are well documented (National Institutes of Health, 2012), especially the bottleneck created for transition into academic careers where the number of available positions is limited. The impact of extended postdoctoral appointments on first full-time, tenure-track appointment and time to first grant (R1) has led to calls for reform in the biomedical sciences workforce (Pickett et al., 2015). What are the long-term benefits of postdoctoral experiences in the biomedical sciences? In terms of salary, evidence suggests that there can be a negative impact. One recent study found that ex-postdocs in the biomedical sciences who remained in the United States after their PhD earned less on average than non-postdocs 10 or more years past degree completion. Women and underrepresented minorities in the biomedical sciences have very different career pathways from majority students (Gibbs Jr. et al., 2014). They found that URM men, URM women, and well-represented women were all less likely to report high interest in faculty careers than well-represented men. In particular, URM women were the most likely to report a high interest in non-research careers relative to all other social-comparison groups they studied in the biomedical sciences. What does this mean for gender- and ethnicity-specific career counseling specifically as it relates to postdoctoral training in the biomedical sciences? As with other studies of this type, retrospective self-reported assessments are subject to recall bias and random sampling limitations, as the authors point out. Research opportunities exist not only to limit these types of sampling and recall effects but also to study how career interests evolve over time within certain disciplines and across identity groups.

Postdoctoral training is important outside the biomedical sciences and even outside science and engineering in general. It may be easy to dismiss the relevance of postdoctoral training in the humanities; however, such programs exist. Early postdoctoral teaching programs were aimed at enhancing the instructional effectiveness of early-stage faculty members, such as those from the Lilly Endowment (Schwen & Sorcinelli, 1983). More recently, limited-term appointments as postdoctoral teaching fellows have developed as transitional training programs from the doctorate to faculty appointments (National Postdoctoral Association, 2017). Several institutions have stand-alone programs that provide their own funding but individual fellowships are available through the Andrew W. Mellon Foundation, for example. There is no direct evidence that graduate students who have gone through these programs are any more successful at finding employment, publishing their scholarly contributions, or being effective teachers. However, there is some evidence that participation of postdoctoral fellows in teaching-development programs as an additional component of their primary research activities has certain benefits in some STEM-based fields (Benbow et al., 2011).

The challenges facing research on postdoctoral training are enormous. They comprise the complexities of research on graduate education, including student tracking, longitudinal study, and defining career success, but with added difficulties ranging from lack of job definition to inconsistent employment categorization. What skills do postdoctoral scholars learn that cannot (or should not) be taught in graduate school? Should there be culminating experiences for postdoctoral training such as a thesis or dissertation in the same way there are for some master's and doctoral degrees? How is career information on postdoctoral training best communicated to graduate students? What are the career benefits that arise from a postdoctoral training experience? This question leads us to what is perhaps one of the most important overarching themes of this monograph: research on career success.

How Is Career Success Defined and Evaluated for Graduates with Advanced Degrees?

This is a research question for more than just the graduate education community but, as it continues to struggle with compatible career preparation, employability, underemployment and unemployment of graduates, justification of federal research dollars in graduate education, and demonstration of the public good from research, this central question must be addressed. Career-outcome studies can be both snapshots and longitudinal exercises. Career data currently are available from selected communities, such as annual reports from the long-standing annual Survey of Doctoral Recipients (SDR) from the National Science Foundation (NSF) (National Center for Science and Engineering Statistics, 2017b), and from individual institutions such as the University of Toronto (Reithmeier et al., 2019). To be of broad value, however, common research questions must be proposed and degree recipients across all disciplines must be longitudinally tracked either by institutions or by an independent organization that can ensure both privacy and high response rates over time. The Council of Graduate Schools recently launched a study funded by NSF, the Andrew W. Mellon Foundation, and the Alfred P. Sloan Foundation to develop tools for institutions to track the career pathways of PhD students. In addition, professional societies like the American Chemical Society (ACS, 2013) have clearly laid out what they believe to be the problems associated with employment opportunities for their graduate students. Whether broad based or disciplinary specific, these reports all have a common conclusion: there are not enough tenure-track faculty positions to accommodate all doctoral recipients. By one estimate (Larson et al., 2014), only 12.8% of engineering PhD recipients will find employment in academia. The study of 10,000 PhD graduates from the University of Toronto cited earlier (Reithmeier et al., 2019) showed that graduates from all disciplines from 2000–15 were employed in the postsecondary education sector at a rate of 51% but only 26% as tenure-track professors. The argument has always been that the remaining majority find jobs in industry. While there is some evidence to support this contention, it is largely unknown where graduates go and what they do for their entire careers across all disciplines. Moreover, career success is distinctly different from (though likely interrelated with) success in graduate school (Patzer et al., 2017) and career outcomes (Tregellas et al., 2018), that is, where a graduate is placed.

To these ends of defining and evaluating career success, new tools and models for surveying degree recipients throughout their careers are being developed, and new and existing databases are being analyzed with these models. Canal-Dominquez and Wall (2014) utilized data from the 2006 Survey on Human Resources in Science and Technology to analyze the careers of roughly 17,000 residents of Spain who obtained their PhD degrees between 1990 and 2006 from a public or private Spanish university. In addition to confirming many of the long-known differences between earnings of PhD recipients by field of knowledge, professional activity, and gender, the study attempts to incorporate qualitative aspects of career success like job satisfaction. Their results suggest that particularly in the private sector, opportunities for advancement and degree of independence are equally as important to perceived job satisfaction as salary. Another career success model comes from the clinician–scientist community (Rubio et al., 2011). As illustrated in figure 14, the model is fed by personal factors such as demographic background (age, gender, race/ethnicity, and socioeconomic status) and psychosocial milieu (life events, stress, dependent care) along with organizational factors such as institutional resources (financial and infrastructure), training (didactic programs, research experience, professional development), relational factors (mentoring and networking), and conflicting demands (scholarly vs. service responsibilities in the academic realm). The measurable career outcomes are extrinsic (publications and reports, leadership positions, and financial success) and intrinsic (job, career, and life satisfaction).

Even as career success is redefined to accommodate metrics from a variety of careers, the academic career path is worthy of continued investigation. Socialization of graduate students for faculty careers has been reviewed (Austin, 2002; Gemme & Gingras, 2012) as have funding efforts geared toward enhancing career paths for graduate students into the professoriate, such as the Preparing Future Faculty (PFF) program (Gaff,

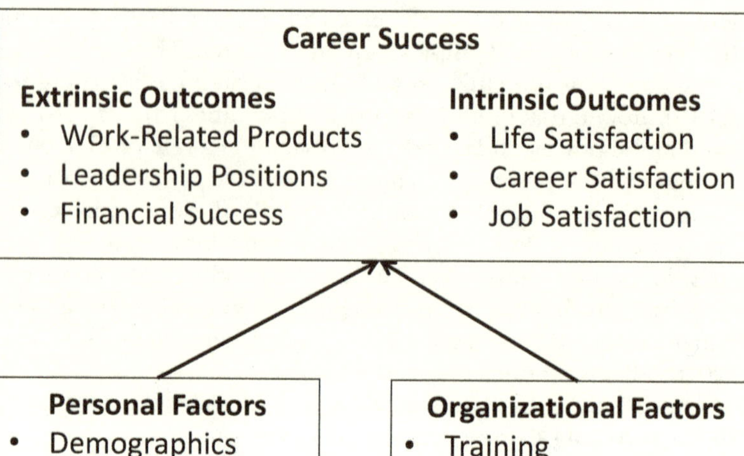

Figure 14. A comprehensive career success model. Adapted from Rubio et al., 2011.

2002; Gaff et al., 2003). The shifting attitudes of graduate students were discussed in the context of the career decision-making process but little research has been performed on the efficacy of training and interventions in the career success of those who enter academic careers. What are the effects of such federal funding programs as the Graduate Research Fellowship (GRFP), Alliance for Graduate Education and the Professoriate (AGEP), and the Faculty Early Career Development (CAREER) programs for example – all from the US National Science Foundation – not only on increasing diversity and productivity in the professoriate but on enhancing the career success of participants over those who did not participate in such programs? Does successful competition for an NSF CAREER award and the individual acclaim it brings translate into a more successful academic career? How is a successful academic career defined and evaluated for those who are in primarily teaching positions compared to those who have high research expectations as part of their job performance? What are the correlations between career success and job retention, especially for academicians from underrepresented groups?

More generally, what career outcomes most broadly represent career success across the widest variety of job functions? For example, publications may be an excellent metric for evaluating the success of advanced degree holders who enter academia; however, what is the equivalent parameter for those in the private sector? How are leadership opportunities defined and are they equivalent across employment sectors? Are opportunities for promotion, advancement, and salary increases equivalent across not only employment sectors but across demographic segments such as gender, race and ethnicity, and age? There are answers to some of these questions; however, the answers change with time and require updating as more advanced models for career success incorporate these considerations. Once developed and validated, how do these models of career success impact programs in terms of enrollment, rankings, and curricular change? As a subset of the research topics on career success, a deeper understanding of the evolution of careers with an advanced degree must be developed – which leads to the final topic of this chapter.

How Do Careers for Those with Graduate Degrees Develop over Time?

A set of research questions related to career success has to do with how careers evolve over time. In addition to the inherent difficulties of conducting any type of longitudinal study on change (Pettigrew, 1990), the lack of an accepted a priori model of career success precludes broad-based studies on career evolution. Nevertheless, successful career pathways for graduate degree recipients can begin to be mapped. This mapping could include qualitative descriptions such as vignettes, case studies, and anecdotes but could also include metrics such as number and timing of promotions, employer transitions, career changes, and life choices. Certainly, a fair amount is known about academic careers of advanced degree holders, particularly with respect to publication records (Wildgaard & Wildgaard, 2018; Zou et al., 2018) but, as pointed out in previous research questions, academic careers are increasingly in the minority for advanced degree holders and involve more than just publication metrics. Nevertheless, even academic careers involve advancement and promotion and can develop into management and administrative positions. The frequency and impact of these transitions in any career can be correlated with training in order to determine how transitions can be positively influenced earlier in the career.

Unexplored questions surround leadership roles of advanced degree holders. A report from the British Council examined the level of educational attainment for 1,709 leaders in the public, private, and non-profit sectors from 30 countries (British Council, 2015). Over half of those surveyed had an advanced degree, including 38% with master's degrees, 22% with professional degrees, but only 9% with a PhD. There are interesting findings related to the demographics and disciplinary backgrounds of the survey participants, including the large percentage of leaders with social-science and humanities backgrounds (55%) and the fact that 46% have had some kind of international experience. In terms of activities that affect leadership skills, this study found qualitative evidence that extracurricular activities contribute to one's career advancement through the establishment of large social and professional networks and the fostering of one's self-esteem. How would these findings fit into the career success model proposed earlier? How are career outcomes like leadership positions defined and incorporated into career success models while allowing for geographic, demographic, and disciplinary differences? Gender equity in leadership is a key area of concern, even within academic institutions (Morley, 2014). How is the development of leadership skills differentially affected by gender, ethnicity, and culture?

Professional societies have some of their own evidence on the development of professional careers. The American Anthropological Association (AAA) surveyed 758 master's degree holders (including those who continued on to obtain a PhD) in a variety of anthropology subdisciplines (Fiske et al., 2010). They found that the most frequent way that respondents found employment was through networking with colleagues or friends. How can networking skills be factored into career success models and how should they be fostered by professional societies? The American Institute of Physics (AIP) focused its report on physicists who had worked in industry for 10 to 15 years past their PhD and found that a small but significant number of the 503 respondents were self-employed. How are the careers for those who work outside of large organizations tracked and mapped? There are certainly other examples, but the point is that professional societies can move beyond descriptive statistics and satisfaction surveys to perform robust longitudinal studies on their memberships that provide direct evidence to advanced degree programs on cause and effect in their training practices. Institutions have similar opportunities. The study from the University of Toronto (Reithmeier et al., 2019) of 10,000 PhD recipients over a decade-and-a-half provides not only important career information for analysis but outlines how this information can be used for program improvement. Similarly, surveys of PhD recipients in the United States are being grouped by time beyond the PhD to better understand the influences of generational and economic differences on the careers of advanced degree holders (Okahana, 2018, 2019).

Whether through professional societies, individual or consortia of universities, federal funding agencies, or governmental organizations, the primary challenges are always related to increasing the number of study participants and successfully tracking them over time. The Survey of Earned Doctorates (SED) is perhaps the largest and most comprehensive data set available in the United States for these types of longitudinal studies; however, to properly align with career success models the appropriate questions must be asked. As described in the previous section on career success, publications are relatively easy to count but identifying and evaluating positions of leadership are more difficult. Appropriate metrics for evaluating leadership positions must be identified. Privacy concerns increasingly prohibit such long-term tracking studies, yet technological advances present unique opportunities to follow individuals simply through information they are already willing to make public on social networks. As mentioned earlier, there are statistical methods for getting at difficult-to-estimate populations (Maltiel et al., 2015; McCormick & Zheng, 2007; McCormick et al., 2010) that must be applied to longitudinal studies on advanced degree recipients. For example, statistics on Indigenous Peoples enrolled in specific graduate degree programs are often suppressed by institutions over privacy concerns. Similarly, data on early-career faculty from underrepresented minorities who do not attain tenure or data on advanced degree holders who put their careers on hold to raise a family are generally not available. There are ways to get at this information. It is in this technological respect that the graduate education community must look beyond its own abilities and engage those most knowledgeable in massive, longitudinal studies to track the career development of advanced degree recipients. There is more on data harvesting in chapter 3.

Research projects on career preparation and success for those pursuing and possessing advanced degrees involve complex, interrelated factors and will require clear definitions, teams of investigators, strong institutional collaborations, and broad-based longitudinal studies. The conclusion to this monograph provides some ideas on how those collaborations might be fostered. First, though, we take a more program- and institution-specific view of research opportunities to improve graduate education at the local level.

3 Graduate Program Improvement

One could argue that if the science of learning at the graduate level, graduate student career preparation, and graduate student success were fully understood, graduate programs would necessarily improve as a result. The converse is true as well. If robust graduate program improvement practices were in place, student learning and career preparation would also improve. However, it is just as important to understand the context in which learning takes place as to understand the learning itself. This chapter is about reframing some of the previous research questions and looking at them from the program level instead of the student level. As with most complex problems, approaching them with simultaneous top-down and bottom-up approaches offers clarity.

Many graduate programs already address program improvement through professional accreditation processes. Graduate-level training in the health sciences, law, social work, and business fall into this category. Those processes are important but are meant to ensure only a minimum standard of excellence. In an attempt to move away from minimum standards and toward continuous improvement, outcomes assessment has permeated much of the accreditation process. Whether through establishing and evaluating specific course-based learning objectives, or through crafting educational and degree program outcomes, the assessment community has impressed upon faculty and administrators alike the importance of defining and assessing student learning beyond course grades and end-of-term course evaluations. Parts of the graduate education community have been slow to adopt outcomes-assessment practices; others have embedded it in their programs at their inception. In the past two decades, however, all have had to implement some form of outcomes assessment to comply with regional accreditation processes (see, for example, the Southern Association of Colleges and Schools "The Principle of Accreditation" [SACSCOC, 2017]) primarily due to the need for public accountability (Jennings Jr., 1989). Professional organization accreditations are an important part of those institutional accreditation processes, often serving as de facto proof of program quality. Again, accreditation processes generally ensure only a minimum standard of acceptability. How do programs continuously improve even when they meet acceptable accreditation standards?

There is a vast body of literature on outcomes assessment that will not be cited here. As a primer, the National Science Foundation publishes a handbook on project evaluation (Frechtling, 2010) to assist its program managers with assessment of educational programs. Its concepts are extensible beyond the STEM disciplines and simple evaluative constructs like the one shown in figure 15 are useful; however, this evaluative schema is not uniformly applied across all graduate programs. In doctoral programs, for example, current practices tend toward performance indicators (rankings, metrics) that combine formative and summative activities. Basic research – in the educational-assessment context – involves more in-depth studies that explore innovative models but is rarely used for decision-making processes. This heavy reliance on performance indicators at the expense of basic research skews policy decisions toward short-term impact at the expense of long-term benefit. For example, perhaps the most well-known program assessment comes from the National Research Council with its quasi-decadal review of US doctoral programs, the most recent of which was published in 2011 (Ostriker et al., 2011). Primarily a program-ranking mechanism, this survey utilizes metrics viewed as most important by program faculty to the quality of a doctoral program, including faculty publications, citations, grants, and awards. To the best of this author's knowledge, no link has ever been established between a mentor's productivity and the advisee's career success, much less skill attainment and educational outcomes. Such a study – even if limited to a single discipline – would be most enlightening. It could tell us, for example, whether commonly used metrics such as number of faculty publications and awards are more important to program and student success than interrelational factors such as the quality of mentorship. Does faculty productivity correlate with program quality, does faculty productivity cause program quality, or is faculty productivity caused by program quality? If not faculty productivity, then what program outcomes are most important and how are they measured?

The program-accreditation function is not meant to provide tools or opportunities to delve deeply into important structural questions surrounding graduate education. To the contrary, those quality-assurance processes only exist because foundational studies provided evidentiary support as to their effectiveness. How is foundational research on the

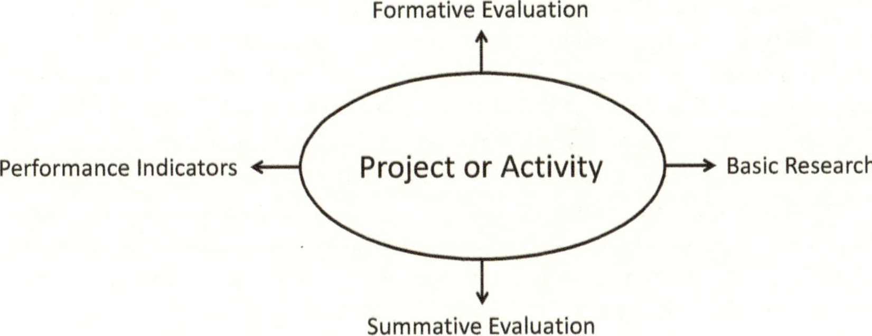

Figure 15. Types of evaluation and assessment activities. Adapted from Frechtling, 2010.

effectiveness of graduate programs conducted in such a way that it not only leads to better accreditation processes but provides programs, schools, and institutions with the necessary tools and evidence to conduct self-evaluations and external reviews?

In short, a better understanding of cause and effect in graduate education is needed not just to satisfy accreditors, auditors, taxpayers, program officers, university presidents, employers, and other constituencies but to satisfy the community of graduate-level educators and researchers. These are perhaps some of the most impactful research questions of the lot because they deal not only with educational ideologies but with practical considerations like resource utilization. The student is the starting point for these considerations and is the focus of the first research question on program improvement.

What Programmatic Factors at Which Stages Influence Graduate Student Enrollment, Retention, and Degree Completion?

The factors influencing an individual's decision to pursue an advanced degree were addressed in chapter 2 in the first research question related to when and why students make this decision. Decisions to remain in a graduate program can also be influenced by personal factors in some instances, although the academic rigors of pursuing an advanced degree play an important role. What are the curricular, programmatic, and cultural influences on graduate student decision-making processes? Some of these factors may be surprising.

In a study of its graduate student population from the University of California, Berkeley (The Graduate Assembly, 2014), the top three predictors of graduate student life satisfaction (comprising positive function, happiness, and well-being) were living conditions, career prospects, and financial confidence. Such factors as overall health, academic engagement, and advisor relationship also played roles in predicting life satisfaction and the propensity for mental health issues such as depression. The role of mental health in all of these discussions should not be underestimated. Another study from the University of California, Berkeley (J. Hyun et al., 2006) found that almost half of the graduate student study participants reported a stress-related problem in the previous year that significantly affected their well-being and/or academic performance. They found that programs and mentors, through such structured activities as orientations and one-on-one advising, can increase awareness of mental health resources on campus and positively impact graduate student well-being. A more recent study from Belgium found that PhD students were at higher risk than other highly educated comparison groups of having or developing psychiatric disorders such as depression (Levecque et al., 2017). Common factors that influence this increased risk include job demands, the supervisor's leadership style, and the decision-making culture. The factors that programs and administrators can positively influence are the focus here, including the admissions, advising, and career-preparation processes.

All stages are worthy of inspection but they can be affected by different institutional policies and programmatic practices. The application process, for example, may be centralized through a graduate school or decentralized at the program level. Admissions decisions are often made at the program level, either as recommendations to a graduate dean or as conveyed directly to the applicant. Similarly, progress to degree may be measured by milestones imposed from above, such as completion of coursework, or from the program itself, such as passing qualifying or comprehensive examinations. These mechanics, while important, are not universally implemented. Although a study on the relative benefits of centralized vs. decentralized graduate education administration would certainly be welcome, it is accepted that institutional autonomy and program ownership are important components of quality assurance such that a "best practices" approach is taken. That is to ask, what information is available about graduate program practices related to enrollment, retention, and degree completion that all programs can use regardless of administrative structure? How can these studies be structured to be less anecdotal and more correlative in their findings? Presentation in chronological order seems appropriate, loosely following the identity-development model of Gardner and others described earlier in figure 2.

The enrollment process comprises three distinct steps: application (here including recruitment), admission, and matriculation. Characteristics such as program quality and institutional prestige may drive prospective student interest; are these the only factors? The graduate education community can use research at the undergraduate level as an example. A recent study (Dale & Krueger, 2014) compared the career earnings of two student cohorts of bachelor students who attended either a highly selective university or a less selective institution. In a straightforward comparison, graduates from highly selective institutions had higher career earnings than those from less selective institutions, reinforcing the prevailing notion that institutional prestige impacts career success. The researchers then compared graduated cohorts who had been accepted to both types of institutions (not necessarily the case in the previous cohort study) but self-selected into their institution of choice based on certain institutional characteristics. In this "self-selection adjusted" analysis, the career earnings difference of graduates from highly selective and less selective institutions went away. Although there was a benefit to students from economically disadvantaged backgrounds attending the more selective institution, overall there was an insignificant payoff to attending a more selective institution for students admitted to both. As illustrated in the earlier career success model, earnings are only one measure of career success. Students attend specific universities for very different reasons, not just career earnings expectations. How would the Dale and Krueger prestige study at the graduate level impact how graduate students are recruited and admitted? Do (or will) program rankings matter as much to prospective students as it is believed and, if so, how? What is the impact of program prestige on earnings for those with advanced degrees?

Institutional prestige also plays an important but different role in the admissions decision process. Graduate admissions decisions are often carried out either in a formulaic way within a graduate school or in a more nuanced way by a small group of people at the program level. Both approaches are often decoupled from financial support decisions; both approaches have their drawbacks. Recent research (Posselt, 2016) shows that in the case of program-based review, admissions decisions are traditionally driven by three perceived measures of merit: undergraduate grade point average (GPA), graduate records examination scores (GRE), and the reputation of the applicant's undergraduate institution. In the case of the PhD, GRE scores (Miller & Stassun, 2014) and undergraduate institutional prestige do not reliably predict degree completion, although they may correlate with other aspects of progress to degree such as first-year grades (Moneta-Koehler et al., 2017) and formal didactic training (Park et al., 2018), or likelihood of academic probation in specific disciplines (Wheeler & Arena, 2009). In fact, one study of 1,800 STEM PhD students at four public institutions in the northeast United States found that men in the lowest quartile of GRE scores completed their degrees at a higher rate than those in the highest quartile of GRE scores (Petersen et al., 2018). A similar result was found outside of North America (Zimmermann et al., 2018) in master's programs. Undergraduate institutional prestige may not predict degree completion and may therefore have limited utility from an admissions standpoint; however, it can play a role in socialization and inequality during graduate school as reflected in the theory of cumulative advantage or the Matthew effect (Gopaul, 2019). Revised admissions methodologies have been developed that use numerical representations of additional factors such as research experience and advanced coursework (Pacheco et al., 2015) as well as interviews, which have long been the standard in healthcare disciplines.

Interviews, letters of recommendation, personality profiles, and other tools for the evaluation of noncognitive constructs are not new to the admissions portfolio (Kyllonenet al., 2005) but, like merit-based review criteria, their utility in predicting success during and after graduate school is mostly unknown (Megginson, 2009). Holistic admissions review (Kent & McCarthy, 2016) is an emergent practice intended to utilize a broad range of factors that may contribute to success in graduate school. It is an evolving practice but currently considers both cognitive and noncognitive evaluations in the admission decision, as well as utilizes standardized evaluation tools such as rubrics to assist in making decisions. Careful studies will be required to measure holistic admissions review effectiveness not only in the admissions process but in improving retention and degree completion. For example, what are the effects of admitting students using holistic review processes relative to using traditional processes (GRE and undergraduate GPA as primary screening tools), especially on student and program success? Do these students fit into the socialization and communities-of-practice theories described earlier in the same way? Are they less or more likely to complete their degrees? Noncompleting students can be an important source of information. Attrition can be the result of academic performance shortcomings but it can also result (at least in part) from inadequate admissions evaluations, improper mentoring, or inflexible administrative procedures that do not address specific student needs.

Once enrolled, these additional factors influence persistence, attrition, and completion. Slightly over half of all students who enroll in a PhD program in the United States complete within 10 years (Sowell et al., 2015).

Comparison with other "150% normal time to degree" completion rates shows that the 10-year PhD completion rate is better than comparable rates in associate degree programs (three-year completion rate) but less than comparable rates in bachelor's degree programs (six-year completion rate) (Kena et al., 2015). Why the doctoral completion rate is so low is a poorly understood phenomenon. Certainly, academic requirements become more stringent for advanced degrees, but other factors are undoubtedly at play.

The Council of Graduate Schools has published perhaps the most comprehensive series of reports on completion and attrition at the doctoral level. The first publication (Council of Graduate Schools, 2004) provides a summary of empirical studies on graduate school completion and attrition before 2004. During that roughly 50-year period, these studies reported attrition rates ranging from 11–68% in various disciplines and institution types. Further detail on completion and attrition rates as a function of discipline, institution type, and cohort size from a survey of 30 participating institutions over a 12-year period was provided by the next monograph in the series (Sowell, Zhang, & Redd, 2008). In the aggregate, 57% of doctoral candidates in this study completed their degrees within 10 years, with completion rates varying from 49–64% depending on field of study. Further demographic breakdown of the survey results by gender, citizenship, and race/ethnicity were highlighted in another report (Sowell, Zhang, Bell, & Redd, 2008), which showed that men, international students, and whites had higher 10-year completion rates than women, domestic students, and non-white domestic students, respectively, in the sample of 41,017 students at 24 participating institutions. The final report (Sowell et al., 2009) provided results and analysis of an exit survey of over 1,400 PhD completers at 18 institutions and found that factors such as financial support and advisor access were keys to completion of their degrees. The importance of financial support on completion and time to degree was further supported in a larger study of 5,000 STEM doctoral programs at 212 US institutions (Zhou & Okahana, 2019). Finally, policy and best-practice implications were the focus of the final report (Sowell et al., 2010), which outlined qualitative findings from 21 participating research institutions in the areas of admissions, mentoring, financial support, research modes, administrative support, and program environment.

Master's-degree completion rates are similarly varied. In the United States, about two-thirds of STEM master's-degree candidates complete within four years, while the four-year completion rate for MBA students is much higher at 86% (Council of Graduate Schools, 2013). One study found that of the Graduate Management Admissions Test (GMAT) registrants, women were 30% less likely to complete the MBA within seven years than men (Montgomery & Anderson, 2007). As enrollments in online master's programs continue to grow, more studies are required to understand the effects of alternative delivery formats on persistence and degree completion across all demographic and ethnic categories. These studies become particularly challenging at the master's level as new degree programs and majors continually emerge. One example is advanced degrees in cybersecurity. These degree programs continue to evolve and receive designated federal funding for scholarships and programs but little is known about how they meet educational and workforce needs, especially for women and underrepresented minorities (Shumba et al., 2013).

Only a handful of systematic studies have been performed on assessing why students do not persist in graduate school and at what stages they are most vulnerable. One study investigated doctoral persistence and completion at a French-speaking Canadian institution using self-determination theory (Litalien & Guay, 2015). The results of this limited study suggest that self-perceived competence and the quality of the student–advisor relationship are the two most important factors in determining persistence in a doctoral program (figure 16). The authors of this study recognized that further research is warranted over longer periods of time that includes more measures than self-reported data. Millett and Nettles (2006) used a conceptual model containing four categories of independent variables to study retention and completion in STEM disciplines. In a fashion analogous to the categories shown in figure 16, the variables are grouped according to observable characteristics (such as student background and admissions criteria) and latent constructs (like student experience in the program and mentoring relationships). Another study examined completion rates in doctoral programs in Norway over a 30-year period (Kyvik & Olsen, 2014). It reported that such factors as improved advisor supervision and introduction of financial incentives to students, advisors, and institutions decreased time to degree and improved completion rates. In the United States, Gittings (Gittings, 2010; Gittings, Bergman, & Osam, 2018; Gittings, Bergman, Shuck, et al., 2018) studied the effects of student attributes and program characteristics on doctoral completion rates at two research universities using Tinto's theory of doctoral attrition (Tinto, 1994) and found that such factors as student age, enrollment status (part time vs. full time), and satisfaction with the research advisor impacted degree completion. In the biomedical sciences there is preliminary evidence that the same factors that can lead to attrition may also manifest themselves as burnout or even mental illness (Nagy et al., 2019). Ehrenberg et al. (2007)

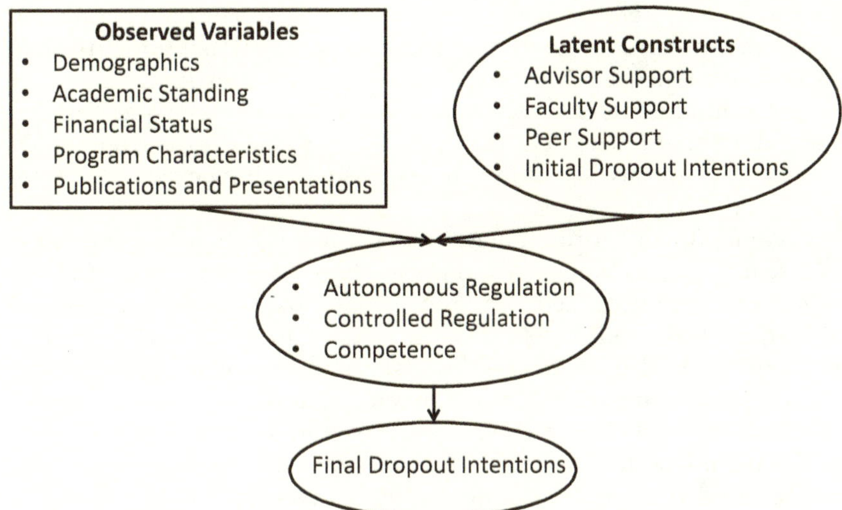

Figure 16. Model of factors from self-determination theory that influence degree program dropout intentions. Adapted from Litalien & Guay, 2015.

studied the program characteristics affecting completion and persistence in the humanities and related fields at 10 US research institutions during the 1990s and the influence of funding from the Andrew W. Mellon Foundation's GEI project on those characteristics. They found that such factors as improved advising, clear departmental expectations on progress toward degree, and a reasonable level of "polish" expected of dissertations all reduced attrition and improved completion rates. There is also much in the literature at the undergraduate level on which to build in the area of such intrapersonal skills as "grit" (Duckworth et al., 2007; Miller-Matero et al., 2018) and "belonging" (Lewis & Hodges, 2015) that have programmatic implications regarding persistence in graduate school.

There is some discipline- and ethnicity-based research on retention and completion. Crede and Borrego (2013) developed a mixed-methods approach to evaluate the experiences of students in three graduate engineering research groups. They proposed that constructs such as international diversity, expectations, climate, organization, individual preferences, and perception of value can be used to evaluate the impact of working in a research group (rather than individually) on degree completion. Differences were also found between international and domestic students at one large, public research institution in the

United States where academic concerns such as career preparation and program structure are more important to international students while social aspects such as advisor relationships may be more important to domestic graduate students. We will see in the next research question that these differences in student populations – especially those from underrepresented groups – span the entire graduate school experience from application to completion.

Completion and attrition may represent one of the most robust areas of research on graduate education. Still, there is room for work. Indeed, others have proposed their own research questions surrounding this issue (McAlpine & Norton, 2006). All of the studies described here are limited in some way: by disciplinary representation, institutional representation, and certainly demographic representation that reflects the time period in which the studies were conducted. How can a wider sample of graduate students be followed and in more discrete time increments (first year, second year, etc.)? How do studies compensate for programmatic heterogeneities that are paramount to differentiation in the field? If this information were made more widely available to prospective and current students, how would it impact their decision-making processes before, during, and after graduate school, if at all? Of all the variables available for study in the areas of student recruitment, retention, and completion, two stand out: student diversity and inclusion. An attempt is made to broach this wide-ranging research topic in the next section.

How Do the Experiences of Students from Underrepresented Groups Differ from Those of Majority Students and Each Other?

The study of factors differentially affecting the preparation, recruiting and admission, education, and career success of students from underrepresented groups permeates all of the research questions posed here. That these issues are grouped into their own research question is a testament to the complexity of the problems and the tenacity with which they persist. The result is an all-encompassing topic with myriad opportunities and needs for specific research projects. It includes the so-called pipeline issues related to preparation for not just graduate school but for college. It includes investigation of inherent biases in the graduate admissions process. It includes campus climates and continuously evolving definitions of what constitutes underrepresentation in one discipline but not another. It also includes in-depth analysis of where and when URM students face unique barriers in graduate school. Even the pipeline analogy has fallen into disfavor because it paints a picture of a common "supply" of students who enter and exit graduate school through a linear, continuous conduit. The "leaky pipeline" carries its own set of negative connotations that benefit neither underrepresented students nor graduate programs. Pipelines have given way to pathways with various "on ramps" and "off ramps," and now to "ecosystems" in graduate education that allow for more synergies and holistic views of the graduate education community. Regardless of analogy or terminology, the preparation for graduate school, the graduate school experience, and the career opportunities for students from varied backgrounds are of continuing interest for students and institutions alike.

The issue of equity in access and admissions is garnering increased scrutiny, not only in the context of landmark Supreme Court decisions (Long, 2015) but with respect to the concept of holistic admissions review (Megginson, 2009). Research in this area is sparse but growing. As described in the previous section, the issue of culture preferences in academic selection was addressed at the program level (Posselt, 2014). Among the findings was a clear inclination by admissions committees to consider racial and ethnic diversity only at the secondary evaluation level; that is, students first had to "make the cut" using traditional evaluative methods such as standardized test scores and undergraduate grade point average; then other considerations were made for the "short list" of applicants. Another recent study (Bersola et al., 2014) examined the doctoral institutional choice process for URM and non-URM students admitted to a selective, research-intensive university in the western United States. Their survey-based findings showed that URM students placed significantly more importance on faculty, student, and community diversity and the cost of living in their decision-making process.

With respect to persistence and completion, there is preliminary evidence (Sowell et al., 2015) that URM students complete doctoral programs at roughly the same rate as majority students but that there is variability in completion rates within the broad category of URM students between Hispanics and Black/African Americans and across STEM disciplines (figure 17). Why these differences exist is the subject of emerging literature.

Burt et al. studied persistence (Burt et al., 2019) and detrimental factors to success (Burt et al., 2018) in Black males – including foreign-born Black males (Burt et al., 2017) – in engineering programs at three US research institutions during 2010–16. In addition to the role of interpersonal relationships, such as faculty advising, to both persistence and nonnormative role strain described elsewhere in this monograph, these investigators begin to explore the interplay between psychosocial strengths (observed from both within and outside the group) and risks (both normative and nonnormative) through

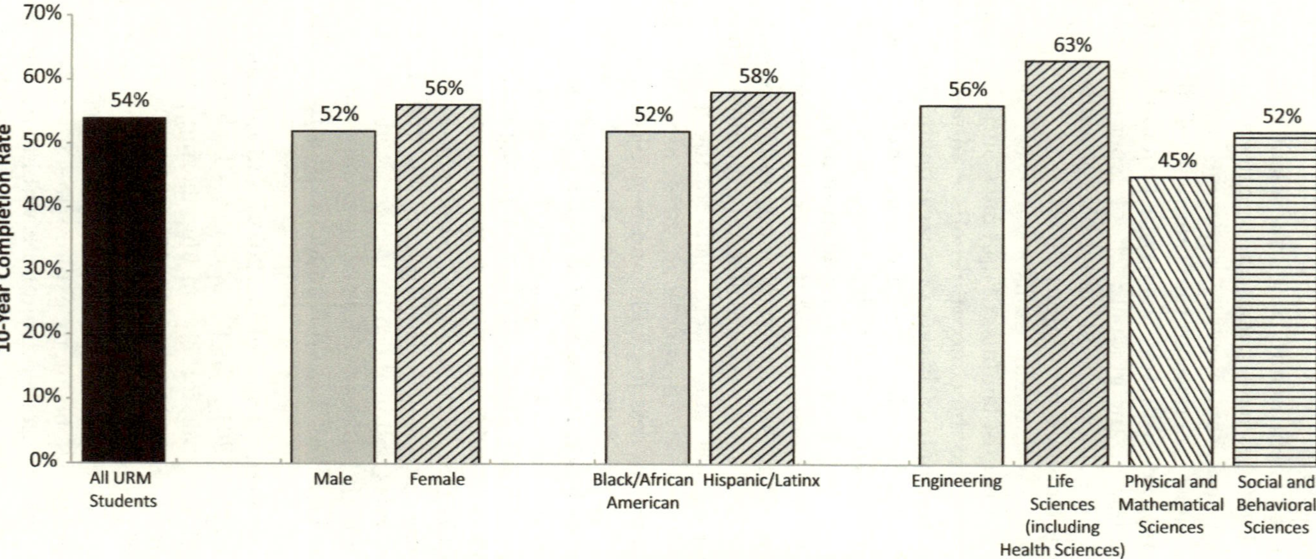

Figure 17. Ten-year doctoral completion rate of underrepresented minority (URM) STEM students. Data courtesy Council of Graduate Schools (Sowell et al., 2015).

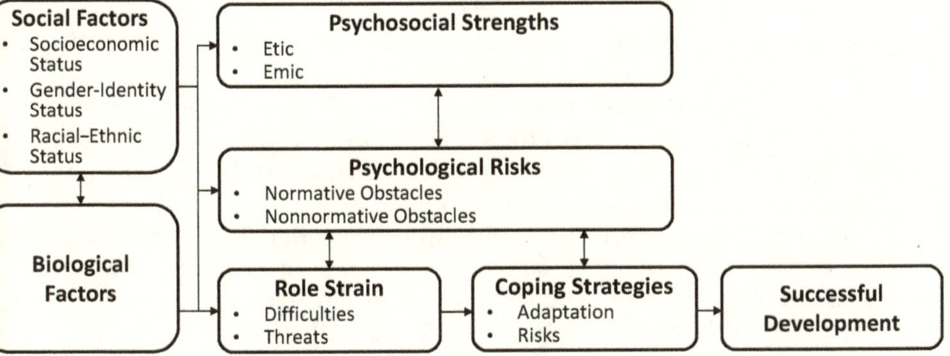

Figure 18. Role strain and adaptation model. Adapted from Bowman, 2006.

application of Bowman's role strain and adaptation model to the graduate school context (Bowman, 2006). As shown in figure 18, an adapted model provides a framework for studying the myriad factors affecting educational and career success for all students. A similar path model identified contributing factors to publication rates and subjective well-being of URM and women doctoral STEM students in the NSF Alliance for Graduate Education and the Professoriate (NSF AGEP) California Alliance (Fisher et al., 2019). Sense of belonging and organizational structure were identified as key factors in publication disparities as has been found in other such studies. Millet and Nettles (Millett & Nettles, 2006) described a survey-based method for evaluating the doctoral experience of US Hispanic students and similarly found that Hispanic students had a lower completion rate than white students, especially in engineering (56% vs. 79%). Their regression analysis showed that, at least in science and mathematics fields, factors such as attending a selective undergraduate institution, full-time enrollment, and attending a private graduate school positively influenced completion rates for their test subjects.

The same factors that affect persistence and completion also affect the decision on whether to go to graduate school for first-generation college students and students from economically disadvantaged backgrounds. As stated earlier, research shows that students who can afford private institutions for their undergraduate experiences are more likely to enter graduate school to pursue advanced degrees (Eide et al., 1998). Is this phenomenon due to financial privilege, superior undergraduate preparation, or other factors? Graduate students from impoverished backgrounds in the social and health sciences have also reported requiring broad support mechanisms – both inside and outside the family element – to reach and complete an advanced degree (Turner & Juntune, 2018). First-generation doctoral students have higher debt loads than non–first-generation graduate students and they rely more heavily on their personal financial resources for support; however, they concentrate in certain disciplines such as education (Gardner, 2013). How do their experiences in graduate school differ as a result?

In addition to ethnic and racial diversity, gender diversity has been an area of concern in certain disciplines for many years. The now decade-old report on Women and Minorities in Science and Engineering authored by the National Research Council (Committee on Maximizing the Potential of Women in Academic Science, Engineering [US], & Committee on Science, & Public Policy [US], 2007) provided an institutional scorecard for tracking the numbers and percentages of women and minorities in faculty ranks in annual, 5-year, and 10-year increments. How have institutions adopted this recommended practice, if at all? A simple statistical sampling of these scorecards with basic analysis would provide useful data to the community on what might be working, even in a narrow employment sector like the STEM professoriate. How does undergraduate debt level differentially affect women, married students, or students with families? A 25-year-old study (Fox, 1992) found that student debt had a slightly larger impact on women's than men's decisions to attend graduate or professional school. How has that changed given that student-loan debt has increased dramatically in the intervening years (Denecke et al., 2016)? One study suggests that the impact of increasing student-loan debt has not changed – students from lower socioeconomic background, students of color, and women continue to bear more of the educational debt among graduate students (Pyne & Grodsky, 2020).

Some researchers have focused on the experiences of women in specific disciplines, especially those related to science, engineering, and mathematics. One author (Herzig, 2004), for example, postulates that doctoral students must become integrated into two sequential yet distinct communities of practice: coursework and research (figure 19). The impact of previously described factors such as funding, confidence, departmental structure, and the job market on persistence of these underrepresented groups in mathematics doctoral programs is described. The concept of self-perceived confidence introduced earlier as a factor in doctoral-program persistence has been suggested as a factor in the motivation for women to pursue academic careers (Evers & Sieverding, 2015). In this study at a large, German university, the self-efficacy variable was studied on academic career intentions using the theory of

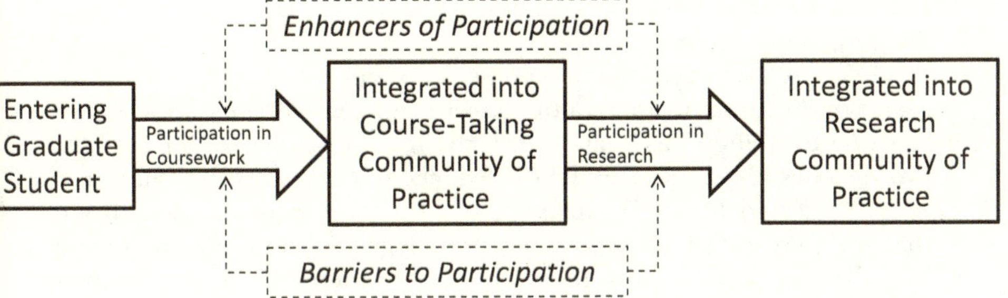

Figure 19. Communities-of-practice model of graduate education. Adapted from Herzig, 2004.

planned behavior. Are the experiences of women in European doctoral programs common in other parts of the world? Are the results the same for women with doctorates who pursue careers outside the academy? Again, these authors cite the limitations of their study and call for further studies to investigate how attitude and subjective norms can be positively influenced to obtain more favorable career outcomes. Recent work utilizing a database of longitudinal information on researchers directly supported by federal grants (UMETRICS [Committee on Institutional Cooperation, 2016]) found that women PhD students at the California Institute of Technology from 2004–9 authored 8.9% fewer papers than men overall (Pezzoni et al., 2016). They also found that student–advisor gender pairing had a measurable influence on publication rates. A more focused study from a large, public research university in the United States found similar results, with publication rate differences by gender most pronounced in the engineering and natural sciences, less pronounced in the humanities and social sciences, and almost non-existent in the education and professional doctoral programs (Lubienski et al., 2018). Publication is only one measure of a student's productivity. How do such factors as gender pairing and gender-biased admissions practices impact the overall student experience, program effectiveness, and career success? One recent comparison of graduate program gender-parity effectiveness between chemistry and civil and environmental engineering programs at two universities between 2009 and 2014 (Posselt et al., 2018) showed a marked difference in result with intentionality – that is, programmatic changes that were made specifically to address the gender-equity issue and program changes that were made for other purposes but ended up affecting gender parity were considered. Such organizational-pathways research is the next step beyond statistics and demographics in understanding how programs can positively institute change.

While the participation of women in science and engineering careers continues to be an area of concern, the percentage of doctorates awarded to women has been on the rise in all disciplines over the past two decades (National Center for Science and Engineering Statistics, 2017b). United States Department of Education projections indicate that the percentage of men entering college will continue to decline over the next decade, with the number of women enrolling in degree-granting postsecondary institutions increasing by 15% and the percentage of men entering such programs growing by only 9% (Kena et al., 2015). One simulation study using historical degree data from the United States between 1970 and 2014 forecasts that women will be the majority of new advanced degree holders by 2035 (Andalib, 2019). Nevertheless, gender biases persist, with men entering faculty careers at higher rates than women even in disciplines where gender parity is increasing (Hughes et al., 2017). What do shifting demographics mean to gender diversity in graduate programs in disciplines like social sciences and life sciences where men are already in the minority on a percentage basis? How can historical biases be overcome even as gender parity is achieved within a discipline?

Finally, studies focusing on promoting representation of and evaluating experiences by graduate students from specific URM subgroups are needed. Even within racial minorities, those attending graduate school at predominantly white institutions (PWIs) face different campus climates and barriers than those at non-PWIs (González, 2019). A common limitation of many of the studies cited here (and even those that are proposed) is that the URM category, no matter how it is defined and how important it is to statistical significance of the work, contains substantial heterogeneities that make broad-based conclusions difficult. Investigations on URM subsets would be useful. In addition to the previous examples, a few such studies exist, though they are primarily experiential reports. For Indigenous Peoples, the concept of "nation building" as opposed solely to graduate study for personal gain can be important (Brayboy et al., 2014). Here practical considerations such as leaving the community to attend graduate school and family support while in graduate school can become career determining. The related concept of cultural capital was used to explore graduate school access for Mexican American graduate students (Espino, 2014). Similar studies for applicants and students with veteran status, underprivileged socioeconomic status, undocumented status, and from the LGBTQ and trans communities, to name just a few, would be important additions to the literature. For example, online survey responses of 91 graduate students (a majority in the United States but also 15 responses from outside the United States) identified safety considerations and misgendering by faculty as key concerns for nonbinary graduate students (Goldberg et al., 2019). There are, of course, many limitations to such voluntary surveys with small numbers of respondents; however, they help raise awareness of the key factors affecting success in the graduate student population. There are also intersections of identity to consider in these studies, for example, students who identify with both LGBTQ and ethnic minority categories. The intersection of underrepresented groups is receiving increased interest. Such intersectional studies are often presented as a further refinement of underrepresented groups, for example, Black female graduate students (Green et al., 2018; Wilkins-Yel et al., 2019), but studies can be broadened as well in order to inform programmatic diversity efforts. Institutional practices and legislative policies have been studied as social boundaries that can affect diversity and inclusion efforts (Posselt et al., 2017), but diversity and equity initiatives themselves can lead to emotional burdens on student participants (Porter et al., 2018). Which is needed more: studies on specific underrepresented subgroups or broader studies on diversity and inclusion efforts? Are these approaches complementary or competitive? Can both types of information be gleaned from larger, longitudinal studies of all graduate students? What about campus climate? Climate surveys are increasingly being employed not only to create more inclusive environments but to influence admissions processes, especially at the undergraduate level. What is the effect of these climate surveys on graduate admissions?

These needs point to the importance of disaggregating data for subgroups both large (women) and in some cases small (Indigenous Peoples). An inherent difficulty in all of these subset studies is the small numbers of participants that are involved. Privacy considerations and statistical validity are but two of the resulting complexities; however, these concerns should not prevent researchers from exploring creative ways of sorting through heterogeneities in URM populations. There are statistical techniques for estimating the size of difficult-to-determine populations (Maltiel et al., 2015; McCormick & Zheng, 2007; McCormick et al., 2010) that can be adapted to advanced degree seekers and holders. The utility of descriptive case studies should not be underestimated for such research. A nuanced understanding of the difficulties certain underrepresented groups face comes first from examples from their communities as described above.

Ultimately, URM graduate student success is a key component of program quality and improvement. How can programs improve their diversity, inclusivity, and climate in light of these career preferences by underrepresented groups? In the broader sense, what are the impacts of holistic admissions review criteria on graduate student quality, programmatic quality, and research productivity? These same questions could be posed for other subsets of the graduate student population, including international students. For example, we have seen that women are less likely to enroll in graduate school in STEM disciplines than men; however, this phenomenon appears more pronounced in domestic applicants than international applicants (Miner, 2019). Why? The differential experiences of international graduate students are the subject of the next research question.

How Do the Experiences of International Students Differ from Those of Domestic Students and What Are the Influences of International Student Enrollment on Graduate Programs?

The trends in international student applications to and enrollment in graduate schools have been tracked for many years through a Council of Graduate Schools annual report (Zhou et al., 2020). Country of origin, field of study, and type of institution in which graduate students enroll have all been tracked over time, allowing for year-over-year percentage change calculations in each of these categories. But the macroscopic factors affecting those decisions, such as immigration policy, geopolitical conflict, pandemics, and global financial markets, not to mention the changing infrastructure in developing countries that cause students to "stay at home" for their graduate education, are not systematically tracked and studied. Nor are international graduate students' experiences differentially monitored during and after graduate school.

Just as in the previous research questions on enrollment, attrition, and persistence in all graduate degree programs, international students leave graduate programs for a variety of reasons. A recent study (Crede & Borrego, 2014) of 685 PhD students enrolled in US engineering programs at four research institutions found that factors such as expectations and project ownership played statistically significant roles in intent to complete the degree. Although the intent to complete in this study was essentially the same irrespective of nation of student origin, the factors influencing that decision varied by student nationality. There are few similar studies across all disciplines or other types of institutions, however, nor is there information on how these factors might be changing with time, especially for students from developing countries. International students are also subjected to racism and discrimination (J. Lee & Rice, 2007); however, little is known about these effects on retention and completion, much less their impact on future international recruiting efforts. The phenomenon of acculturational homophily – specifically, English-name usage – by a sample of US graduate students who obtained their undergraduate degrees in China suggests that name assimilation can have positive socioeconomic outcomes (Xu, 2017). The socialization perspective of the international graduate student population has been described in the context of second-language training (Okuda & Anderson, 2018), peer interactions (S. Hyun, 2019), and communities of intercultural practice (Zhang, 2018). As in these studies, much of the focus is on graduate students from China; however, little research has been performed by grouping country of origin by cultural difference rather than specific country. The cultural difference approach is widely used at the undergraduate level to assess learning and outcomes from study-abroad experiences in different cultural settings yet is used not at all in the reverse direction at the graduate level. Are there commonalities in socialization, communities of intercultural practice, and advisor relationships between students from countries with similar cultural differences?

Another cause for concern is the lack of research on how international students best learn and what enculturation and mentoring activities positively influence not just completion rate but research productivity, professional skills development, and – ultimately – career success. As discussed earlier, mentoring plays an important role in the success of graduate students both during and after graduate school. In one study of 367 international graduate students at the University of Florida, the Advisory Working Alliance Inventory (AWAI) model of advisor–advisee relationships was adapted to include two additional factors identified as unique to the international advisee–advisor relationship: cross-cultural empathy and financial support (figure 20). They found that financial support – while important to all graduate students – may have different importance and implications for international students. They also suggested further research questions, including disaggregating cultural variations by geographic and disciplinary boundaries. Financial support has additional implications, including immigration status, for international students. This strong influence of financial support on international students has been shown to influence how they perceive their relationship with advisors (Cantwell et al., 2018). As an international student nears degree completion, the decision to seek employment in one's country of origin or remain in the country of graduate education is influenced by many factors. One qualitative study suggests that information provided by career services has a strong influence (Shen & Herr, 2004). So-called stay rates of US temporary visa holders upon completion of

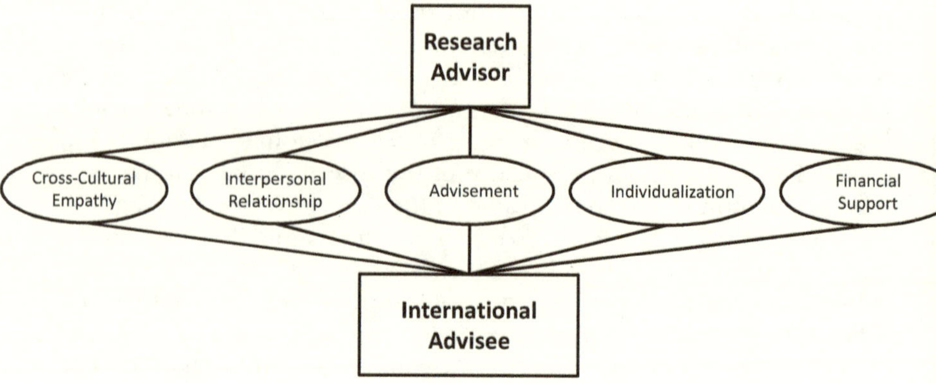

Figure 20. Factors affecting the advisor–advisee relationship for international graduate students. Adapted from Rice et al., 2009.

their graduate degrees have increased between 10% and 20% over the past two decades (National Center for Science and Engineering Statistics, 2017b), but the influence of factors beyond program, institutional, and employer control, such as federal immigration and employment policies, is largely unknown.

There is limited information on the workforce impact international students have in selected disciplines. A 2005 report by the National Academies on the impact of international graduate students and postdoctoral scholars in the United States (National Research Council, 2005) provides evidence of positive contributions on economic impact and innovation from international students in the STEM disciplines upon degree completion. It also provides additional data on graduate stay rates and makes recommendations on how immigration and foreign policy can be shaped to enhance the influx of international students to graduate programs. It notes, however, that little is known about the career paths of these students. The ongoing joint project by the Organisation for Economic Co-operation and Development (OECD), UNESCO Institute for Statistics, Eurostat, and the National Science Foundation to develop internationally comparable indicators of the career paths and mobility of doctorate holders continues to produce reports both on methodology (Auriol et al., 2012) and study results, including labor market impact (Auriol et al., 2013) and on intercountry mobility of research scientists (Appelt et al., 2015). Researcher mobility has implications for the country of education and the country (or countries over one's career) of employment (Regets, 2001). Compounding the difficulties of studying researcher mobility and career success is the problem of student tracking. International students who leave their country of graduate education can be difficult to track – sometimes of their own volition – especially in countries where government censorship is most pervasive.

International students are such an important aspect of graduate education program effectiveness that a separate investigation is warranted. Many of the research questions posed here could have a subset of studies devoted solely to comparative analysis of domestic and international students, which could be further divided by country of origin and discipline. There are also intersections of the international student population with other groups of interest, for example international women and ethnic minorities within and across international populations. As a further example, Canadian and US institutions could cooperate to study any of the graduate education research topics suggested here for Indigenous Peoples with ethnic or cultural similarities who may be differentially classified as international or domestic students simply because of country of origin and enrollment. Not only might their training be different due to institutional variations but there might be practical considerations like access to funding and support that could have profound effects on their experiences. The specific topic of funding and support leads to the next topic.

How Does the Funding Mode (or Combinations of Modes) Affect Graduate Student Outcomes?

> I think you may say we have almost reached the point when every person who received the Ph.D. degree in the United States has held an appointment (i.e., a scholarship, an assistantship, or a fellowship) every year of his work as a graduate student.
>
> – George Barnett, Johns Hopkins University
> at the 1917 AAU meeting (Berelson, 1960b)

As this quotation from 100 years ago illustrates, funding has always been inextricably linked with discussions on the purpose and importance of graduate education. Interestingly, the primary modes of graduate student support have not changed in the past century: scholarships, fellowships, assistantships (research, teaching, graduate), and self-support. The sources of those funds have certainly evolved, especially with respect to federally funded fellowships and more recently university-endowed fellowships. As a result, both parts of the funding equation (dollars and their impact) require continued analysis. A periodic report from the National Center for Science and Engineering Statistics (NCSES) (NCSES, 2017a) provides some basic longitudinal information on funding modes at the doctoral level. Doctoral students in the humanities rely heavily on teaching assistantships as their primary source of financial support in graduate school, while their counterparts in the physical sciences are funded primarily on research assistantships or traineeships. Fellowships and traineeships, on the other hand, constitute the majority of financial support for graduate students in the life sciences whereas students obtaining education research doctorates are primarily self-funded. Women receive a higher percentage of fellowships than men in the aggregate (National Center for Science and Engineering Statistics, 2017b) but also utilize spouse's, partner's, or family's earnings or savings more substantially than men. Funding sources are, of course, fluid. Even students who receive prestigious fellowships may need secondary sources to support their education at some point. Assistantships, traineeships, and fellowships often last for a maximum of five years, which is below the median time to degree in all US doctoral disciplines (National Center for Science and Engineering Statistics, 2017a). Unionization of teaching and even research assistants is an important topic at some institutions but not others. The impact of graduate student unionization was covered in the literature over 10 years ago (Julius & Gumport, 2003; Lafer, 2003; J. Lee et al., 2004) but has seen little new research since. How has unionization improved working conditions for graduate students in the intervening years? Do graduate students with degrees in right-to-work states have different career paths from those in unionized states? What are the influences of graduate student unionization on program quality?

Even less is known about how the funding method(s) affect graduate student success during and after graduate school. There is much discussion on the relative merits of directly funding people (fellowships) vs. funding projects (assistantships) vs. a hybrid approach (traineeships). There are strong opinions on all sides of this discussion but little empirical evidence – with some notable exceptions described below – to fully support any of the positions. What are the effects of not only funding mode but funding source on graduate student success? Is the level of support (annual stipend) more important than the duration of the support (three vs. five years)? What is the impact of unpaid internship requirements on attrition and time to degree? Does five years of guaranteed support increase or decrease time to degree? Research (now decades old) at one US research institution (Ehrenberg & Mavros, 1995) found that the type of financial support a student receives does affect completion rate, attrition, and time to degree; however, only four disciplinary fields were studied, only one of which was non-STEM. Another investigation of graduate student funding in the STEM fields utilizing data from the Survey of Earned Doctorates from the National Science Foundation (Knight et al., 2018) found significant differences in funding portfolios between STEM subdisciplines as one might expect, as well as further differences within the fields that do not necessarily correlate with institutional factors. Outside the STEM disciplines, analysis of the Graduate Education Initiative from the Andrew W. Mellon Foundation (Groen et al., 2008) found that in the humanities disciplines they financially supported and studied, financial aid had a larger positive impact on time to completion than it did on persistence. Even those cohorts with generous financial-aid packages had high attrition. Have program changes been made as a result and, if so, what has been their effect? A recent study of 3,092 doctoral candidates in a variety of fields at a Belgian research university (van der Haert et al., 2014) showed that those with prestigious fellowships had the highest 10-year completion rates, whereas those with no financing had the lowest. Those on assistantships and research contracts had completion rates intermediate to those two funding extremes.

In the United States, graduate student financial support from the National Science Foundation and the National Institutes of Health are two sources from which studies are starting to emerge. For example, results from ongoing analysis of NSF's Graduate Research Fellowship Program (GRFP) fellows through the years suggest that prestigious, nationally competitive fellowships like the GRFP increase the likelihood of completing the PhD within a specified 10-year time period across a variety of STEM disciplines but do not significantly influence average time to degree (Goldsmith et al., 2002). More recent results suggest that at least in the life-sciences disciplines, GRFP awards increase the production of publications (Graddy-Reed et al., 2016). Other studies on the GRFP also report positive influences on fellow research productivity as well as employment status (Bartolone et al., 2014); however, no analysis on intrinsic measures of subsequent career success – especially outside of the professoriate – was performed. The availability of these awards is uneven, however, as institutional factors, such as whether the institution is public or private and size of the program, can influence the likelihood of receiving an award (Graddy-Reed, Lanahan, & Ross, 2017). The authors of this study identify a number of key institutional factors for further study, including the impact of faculty-advisor research productivity on the probability of their advisee's success in national funding competitions such as the GRFP. Even further, what are the effects of advisor research productivity, institutional reputation, and program size on the career success of their graduates? In the biomedical sciences, recent studies related to funding for PhD students from the National Institutes of Health suggest that trainees and fellowships have a more direct influence than research assistantships on full-time enrollment levels but that enrollment grows disproportionately for US citizens and permanent residents compared to enrollment growth for international students (Blume-Kohout & Adhikari, 2016). This same study of NIH-funded doctoral students in the biomedical sciences also shows that international students are more likely than domestic students to take postdoctoral positions and that domestic students supported primarily on research assistantships have a higher probability of taking a research-related job in the United States as compared to those supported by traineeships or fellowships. These results have implications for the workforce needs discussed in the next research topic but, at this time, little is known about how funding mechanisms influence graduate student skills development even in STEM fields. What are the effects of funding mechanisms on graduate student productivity beyond publications? What is the productivity of graduate students at institutions that do not receive substantial federal funding relative to those that do? What are the long-term impacts of the various funding mechanisms on student debt, employment opportunities, and career success?

Even less is known about how students in the non-STEM disciplines fare absent national fellowship programs or federally funded, project-based research assistantships. What would the two-decades-old study described earlier (Ehrenberg & Mavros, 1995) on financial support in disciplines such as economics and English look like today? What would it look like if all disciplines were evaluated? With the emergence and growth of institutionally funded fellowships across all disciplines, universities must be able to justify the use of scarce internal resources for graduate education. As institutions move to self-reporting of financial-support statistics for transparency and accountability efforts (see the University of Washington Graduate School [2015], for example), broader correlations between funding mode, time to degree, persistence, and career success will become possible. What happens if these funding sources dry up? How are institutional resources for graduate student financial support best managed – as separately endowed funds, from tuition revenue, or from a centralized budget? Not only are these broad-based, comprehensive funding studies needed but so are agreed-upon definitions, standards, and repositories for collecting and analyzing these data. This correlative research should precede policy discussions, not trail them. So, too, should research on the employment opportunities graduate students face and how programs should (or should not) respond to short-term projections. This is the topic of the next section.

How Should Graduate Programs Respond to Changing Workforce Needs?

This particular research question is meant to bring focus to the most fundamental of them all, namely, "What is the purpose of the graduate degree?" While ultimately important, the question is more rhetorical than an actionable research topic, so the challenge in developing the corresponding subset of research questions is to somehow link what graduate students learn with what they ultimately do in their long careers. A logical place to start is with employers. Do the skills outlined in chapter 1 adequately prepare students for the careers they face? Do they correlate with the skills employers seek? How should the skills employers desire inform the development, implementation, and evaluation of professional development skills described earlier? These questions are not new. Here is another excerpt from the 50-year-old *Nature* article cited earlier:

> [U]niversities should ask themselves whether the pattern of graduate education in the United States to which everybody is accustomed is really the best suited for the modern world. The way in which employers (or potential employers) have taken to complaining of the over-specialization of the products of the graduate schools (Labour market: Bread lines for physicists, 1970) is one sign that change may be called for. (Are graduate students worth keeping? 1970)

One approach is to first take an inventory of what graduate degree holders actually do in their careers. There have been several reports on career skills, mostly from the perspective of workforce development. A recent report from the Research Councils UK and the higher education funding bodies for England and Wales attempted to document the value of doctorate holders to employers (Diamond et al., 2014). Employers cited such transferable skills as problem solving, research and analysis, and an ability to communicate complex information as strengths of doctoral graduates. But they also cited relevant work experience and evidence of other skills as being important in the hiring process. Similar skill sets were identified by employers as important to "employability" in a study of master's-level students at one Canadian institution where students participated in a work term as part of the degree program (Chhinzer & Russo, 2018). The issue of how one defines employability for these purposes aside, they found that employers valued professional maturity, interpersonal skills, and communication skills when evaluating employability. There is even concern in some countries that advanced degree holders – especially those with a PhD – are overeducated (overskilled and/or overqualified) for the jobs they are performing (Ermini et al., 2017).

There have also been disciplinary-based approaches to career inventories. For example, the American Institute of Physics (AIP) released a study of physicists who earned their PhDs 10 to 15 years earlier (Czujko & Anderson, 2015). It grouped respondents by general career classification, including eight categories in the private sector such as finance, industry (non-STEM), and self-employed. It found that among those working in the private sector, over 85% of respondents reported using the cognitive skill of "ability to solve complex problems" "frequently" in their jobs, while an even higher percentage cited using the interpersonal skill of "working on a team" frequently. In a related study of master's degree holders in archeology (Fiske et al., 2010), the American Anthropological Association found that among workplace-preparation skills, over three-fourths of the 758 respondents (the majority of whom are in applied anthropology or archeology) ranked technical writing for proposals and grants as the most important skill for the master's curricula. More broadly, a study of 2013 National Survey of College Graduates data reveals that 60% of STEM master's degree holders report working in a job closely related to their degree, whereas a similar percentage of non-STEM master's degree holders report working in areas not related to their degrees (Okahana & Hao, 2019). Specific skills and employer perceptions were not addressed in this study. In the biomedical sciences, a recent study on the effects of budget expansions at the US National Institutes of Health in the early 2000s suggests that prospective students do respond to apparent workforce needs through increases in first-time enrollments but that they do not consider how those needs might evolve upon degree completion (Blume-Kohout & Clack, 2013). Further, these researchers found that neither availability of NIH funding nor current relative wages in the biomedical workforce influence six-year completion rates. Within the sub-discipline of biomedical data science, the US National Institutes of Health implemented a Big Data to Knowledge (BD2K) pre-doctoral training program to address the perceived workforce need for biomedical scientists trained in data science; however, one analysis (Dunn & Bourne, 2017) indicates that the program is undersubscribed due to factors such as limited demand and immaturity of data-science training programs. Similar studies on the interplay between workforce needs, availability of funding, and skills development are needed in all disciplines, not just STEM.

Further input is needed from private-sector employers, university administrators, and technology leaders on their perspectives of skill balance in the advanced degree holder. This information then needs to be used by degree programs to optimize the balance of cognitive and noncognitive skills development they offer to their students. The result would be an ability to map emerging requisite workplace skills with core competence to create programs that are flexible enough to meet the needs of current and future students. As described earlier in the context of workforce preparation and skills development, not only are these definitions complex but the implications for the number and size of graduate programs in these areas is profound. Discussions on program viability and size – whether carried out by individual institutions or professional societies – should be informed by data, not just in the historical sense of what students from these programs have done with their careers but also in terms of what they could do with their careers as society and the workforce evolve. The need for such data brings into focus the next topic of research: reliable data and how to access it.

How Do Researchers Link across Data Sets to Take Full Advantage of the Wealth of Information Available (or That Will Be Available) on Graduate Education?

A 1995 US National Academies Report on reshaping STEM graduate education (Committee on Science, Engineering, and Public Policy, 1995) recommended establishing a national database to house information on career tracks, time to degree, placement rates, and financial aid for use by prospective students and program faculty. That recommendation was reaffirmed and strengthened in its most recent report over 20 years later (National Academies of Sciences, Engineering, and Medicine, 2018). Still, no such database exists and the need persists across all disciplines. As new research projects and methodologies are developed, the incorporation of existing data into ongoing activities must also be addressed, as well as how best to make findings available to others to use in their own studies. What are typical starting salaries for advanced degree holders by gender, ethnicity, country of origin, discipline, and institution type? Are they working in the areas in which they are trained? What is the median time between jobs? How often do advanced degree holders change jobs in their careers? What, if any, are the differential long-term benefits of obtaining a doctorate over a master's degree in certain fields? Do advanced degree holders participate in community service, philanthropic activities, and institutional giving at higher rates than baccalaureate degree holders? Institutions may have the answers to some of these questions (and may guard them as corporate secrets), but how can the graduate education community advocate for itself without system-level data?

In this respect the research projects that may stem from these questions will generate new knowledge as does any other scholarly investigation. The results should be disseminated in similar fashion to those scholarly works, including new methods for data exchange (Haak et al., 2012) and broader utilization of the internet via science gateways (K. Lawrence et al., 2015). The involvement of information scientists is desperately needed to provide the tools for workflow analysis of divergent sets of data ranging from student-level information to global research workforce databases. Emergent analysis of ubiquitous social-media content can be used in myriad ways, including specifics of program improvement such as attrition (Berdanier et al., 2020). In a manner analogous to the iPlant Collaborative developed to provide cyberinfrastructure in support of plant-biology research (Goff et al., 2011), the data generated from these research projects on graduate education should be coupled with results from other educational-psychology and related projects at all educational levels in order to form a comprehensive view of education that is widely available to all researchers in these fields. Some nascent attempts at collecting longitudinal data are underway, such as the UMETRICS project cited earlier (Committee on Institutional Cooperation, 2016). Unfortunately, these data reflect only a handful of institutions and come from tracking students whose funding comes only from federal sources. Similarly narrow in scope but of a different approach are federally funded data centers aligned with specific funding programs, such as the Coordination and Evaluation Center (CEC) at the University of California at Los Angeles, which collects and analyzes data for three programs that support graduate-level training. In all cases, key difficulties will be protecting student privacy in the collection of student-level data and a common framework for submitting requisite institutional data. The technology exists to address these concerns but funding and appropriate oversight are necessary.

The need for more and better data sets, longitudinal research, and research collaborations encapsulates the challenges facing the graduate education community as it seeks to improve its degree programs. These are the same barriers that inhibit foundational research on student learning and career preparation. In this chapter and the two that preceded it, an attempt has been made to outline research questions that will further knowledge generation in these important areas of graduate education. The remaining questions – those of who should financially support and coordinate these research efforts beyond the individual programs – are the subject of the conclusion.

Conclusion

Proposing a research agenda is easy enough. Executing it is quite another matter. The difficulties and complexities of pursuing these research topics are not lost upon this author. Indeed, substantial changes in funding structures, oversight bodies, and member organizations in which the author has participated may be required to implement some of the studies proposed here. But change can happen and is often advanced by key findings that accelerate the process. The final research topics, then, are meant to stimulate conversation in the graduate education community and beyond as to where and how these ground-breaking foundational studies might be carried out and how long-term, longitudinal research with clear goals and objectives can be supported.

Which Methodological Approaches Are Best Suited to Exploring These Research Questions?

We have come full circle; that is, we reconsider the type of research needed to better understand graduate education and all of its outcomes. Hopefully, it is more evident than before that more foundational research is needed across the spectrum of graduate education, but the question of how that research should be carried out remains. In the introduction, various approaches were outlined in the context of the educational research paradigm wars of interpretive vs. causal investigations. We have seen examples of both types of research in the course of this monograph. Again, both can be useful but in different ways. The interpretive studies help us make sense of the arrays of data that we can collect. They help us identify potential causal studies and form hypotheses to test. In terms of foundational research, however, the causal studies are most needed. They help us shape policy and implement program improvements that directly benefit students and their careers.

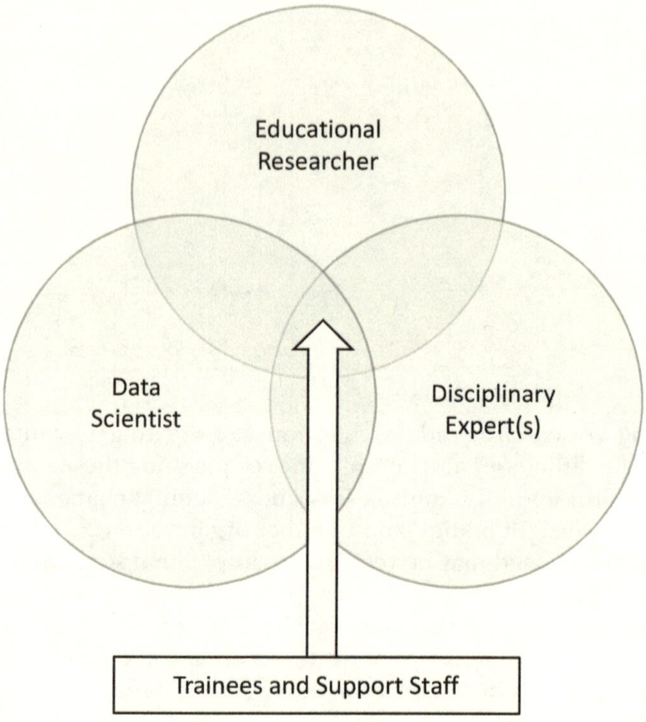

Figure 21. Example of a collaborative graduate education research team.

As important as the research approach is the research team. One observation in compiling the literature necessary for this monograph is that – with a few more reçent and notable exceptions – the research teams are too narrow in their collective skill sets. This is not a criticism of the individuals; rather, it is an inherent weakness of how most research is funded and executed. One example of how a graduate education research team might be constituted is given in figure 21. The educational researcher has broad perspectives on learning theories, pedagogy, and human development. The disciplinary experts provide much-needed access to individuals and data sets as well as bring much-needed context to the formation of the studies and interpretation of results. The data scientists are experts in the collection and interpretation of ever-increasing amounts of information. While one person could certainly possess all the necessary expertise, we have seen examples in previous sections where attempts to train disciplinary experts in data science and informatics proved unsuccessful (Dunn & Bourne, 2017). The number and background of contributors and specialists can vary, of course, but these three areas of expertise represent a minimum for an adequate interdisciplinary team. The contributions of the trainees and support staff should not be underestimated. Not only do they perform the majority of the work but they represent the next generation of cross-trained researchers who can impact how this research is organized and conducted in the future. What special skill sets are missing in this model? Certainly, the data sets could exist or easily be gathered from student demographics or program outcomes, but don't forget the examples given in the monograph of how simulations now permeate graduate education research. Simulations allow researchers to explore "what-if" scenarios as well as conduct research on small populations within the larger graduate education community that cannot be examined due to statistical limits of small numbers, privacy concerns, or insufficient information. What kind of research team, for example, would be required to run simulations on career outcomes of LGBTQ master's students in creative writing? It is not possible to collect all of the information necessary to perform the research outlined here, especially from a longitudinal standpoint. Simulations can fill in the gaps of knowledge left from incomplete data collection.

In an ideal world, the evidence provided by these foundational studies from interdisciplinary teams would be used by administrators and policy makers to shape programs at all levels of engagements. This evidence-based approach to policy making would ensure that students obtain the appropriate graduate-level skills for the corresponding degree. That they then had successful careers based upon those skills would be a clear indicator that the degree program was of high quality. The link between skills and career outcomes is complex and involves many factors beyond a program's control, however, and even a deeper understanding of graduate-level teaching and learning will not by itself lead to improved careers. So, the final research topic is based upon an organizational view of graduate education that evolves from the program level, moves up through the institutional level, and eventually ends with the organizations and communities that are dedicated to improving graduate education at the national and international levels.

Who Is Responsible for Graduate Education Improvement and How Is Change Best Implemented When Necessary?

The gatekeepers for graduate education reside at the program and departmental levels. Here the faculty and administrative staff toil with the mountains of applications, individual and institutional complexities of student enrollment, assessment of scholarly accomplishment, and tracking of their graduates but their roles are not formalized across institutions (Wiener & Peterson, 2019). They have direct access to much of the important information needed to carry out the research topics proposed in this monograph but they often lack the time, resources, institutional support, and even research expertise necessary to do so. Further, they may not possess the broader perspective that comes through their corresponding professional societies or across disciplines and beyond their own institutions. To be sure, some findings are shared by these gatekeepers through presentations at regional or national meetings of professional societies. The content of these presentations can be highly anecdotal, however, and may not be relevant to all institutional types or beyond the discipline. This observation is not to minimize their importance. As mentioned in the introduction to this monograph, creative discovery is one way of advancing a field and when unique program characteristics are found to be effective, they should be shared with a wider audience. That sharing of information should be the first step in program improvement, not the last.

How can departments and programs working under heavy resource constraints carry out effective research of their own that will be of maximal impact and relevant beyond their microenvironment? There are several questions to consider further. First, does the project have the support of the appropriate higher administration units, including school and institutional levels? Even if formal approval is not required to carry out analysis of program-level data, such buy-in can provide resources that can make the study more impactful. Second, can the program team with other units to create more robust data sets and more meaningful analyses? Such cooperation could be between two or more units within or across a school, or between similar departments in a common geographic region or at peer institutions. Third, what unique information can be generated? Departments and programs often concern themselves with routine information on numbers of applicants, numbers enrolled, numbers graduated, and traditional metrics of quality such as grade point average and standardized test scores. What does the program know about accepted applicants who chose to go to another institution? Where did they go and why did they go there? What happens to enrolled students who do not complete their degrees? A number of research topics were raised related to retention and attrition in chapter 3. Departments and programs have access to much of this information. Where do graduates go and what do they do? These are the issues of career success and longitudinal studies that permeate many of the research questions. What is the program's definition of career success? What ways are most effective for tracking and engaging with alumni and alumnae? Finally, how are the findings best disseminated? Regional conferences are convenient and even preferable for some studies, but there should be a higher scholarly purpose to these studies. Again, simple comparative studies are often more meaningful than descriptive statistics alone. Are there society technical journals that would accept a publication on graduate education? If not, why not? Journal editors and editorial boards have an important role to play in bringing research on graduate education into context with their journal's technical content. We have seen examples of disciplinary engagement in graduate education reform by professional societies, such as the American Historical Association (Grafton & Grossman, 2011) and the American Chemical Society (ACS, 2013). Even then, such recommendations are viewed in the context of the local department or program (Ashby & Maher, 2019). How can calls for change from the national or international level be implemented at the program level?

At the institutional level, many of the same questions and barriers from the program level apply; however, there are other opportunities. Typically, graduate education research projects are initiated in the graduate school or similar centralized administrative oversight unit. Institutional responsibility for and participation in graduate education research should extend beyond the graduate school, however. A university's institutional research unit should be heavily invested in the generation, evaluation, and dissemination of these research projects, as should their offices of assessment (if separate from institutional research), career placement, international programs, student life, and school of education. These administrative units can foster the collaboration of highly skilled researchers from across the university. For example, they can facilitate projects that involve researchers from schools of education with those from arts and sciences, or between business, law, and medicine. A single graduate assistantship or funds for hourly researchers from a centralized graduate education unit like a graduate school can pay enormous institutional benefits.

These centralized administrative units are also often responsible for program reviews. Are the right questions being asked and the appropriate metrics being employed? Institutional policies on such emerging practices as holistic admissions review and program outcomes assessment influence how programs and departments think about graduate education. With respect to outcomes assessment, a few institutions have published program outcomes for their graduate degree programs, along with the methodology on how periodic evaluations are performed and how those degree-program outcomes are being met. The Graduate

School at Oregon State University, for example, has the following outcomes for all PhD programs published on its website (Oregon State University, 2016):

> the student shall:
> (a) produce and defend an original significant contribution to knowledge;
> (b) demonstrate mastery of subject material; and
> (c) be able to conduct scholarly activities in an ethical manner.

These program outcomes were developed and approved by a graduate faculty governance body and are assessed at the program level. Assuming the appropriate assessment and evaluation information are available, questions of accountability and responsibility arise. Presumably the same people who decide upon the program outcomes and how to assess them are involved in implementing the change necessary to improve deficiencies. But this is not always the case. Administrators allow poorly performing programs to persist. Students continue to enroll in programs that may not optimally meet their career objectives. New graduate degree and certificate programs are created with no milestones, sunset provisions, formative evaluation strategies, or attention to scholarly rigor. At the other end of the quality spectrum, top-performing program characteristics may be difficult to replicate at other institutions. How are programs to improve? Who should implement change? The so-called local control that graduate programs and faculty enjoy is both an asset and a liability when it comes to implementing change (Leshner & Scherer, 2019).

Organizational change in institutions of higher education is a well-researched area. Entire graduate degree programs are dedicated to this topic, key among them higher education administration. But many of the theories on institutional change in higher education were developed over two decades ago (Tierney, 1988) or have not been fully tested; even the evolving topics of globalization and internationalization are more than a decade old (Enders, 2004; Vaira, 2004). What is new in the fundamentals of institutional change? Simulations are beginning to emerge, such as modeling of research universities for the effects of such factors as declining international graduate student enrollments and online professional master's programs on research activities (Rouse et al., 2018). There is tremendous variation in how institutions of higher education operate worldwide, so it follows that reform and change will vary as well. The concerns over higher education reform in North America, most of Europe, and Oceania are different from those in sub-Saharan Africa,

South America, and central and east Asia (Gornitzka et al., 2005; Kogan & Bauer, 2006; Shin et al., 2018). Higher education reform in Europe is fairly well documented but changes evolving from the Bologna Process and Lisbon Agenda are primarily targeted at the bachelor's level (Jacobs & van der Ploeg, 2006). What changes are evolving in European higher education at the post-graduate level? What can countries learn from one another? Is Germany's Excellence Initiative and Excellence Strategy (especially the graduate school component) (Deutsche Forschungsgemeinschaft, 2020) translatable outside the European Union? Is it time for a world congress on graduate education and, if so, who will take the lead? This is where higher-level cooperation on graduate education research is needed.

One approach is through multi-institutional networks. These could be international networks but, more commonly, they are disciplinary networks with membership limited to domestic or allied institutions. This limitation in participation is due in no small part to funding mechanisms, which will be described in a moment. One such North American collaborative network in the STEM disciplines is the Center for the Integration of Research, Teaching, and Learning (CIRTL). The CIRTL network has 38 research-university members whose primary mission is to improve undergraduate STEM education through the preparation of effective college instructors. As a result, there is a graduate education component to their work. As illustrated in figure 22, the potential impact of these network structures comes in the form of collective gains in knowledge, resources, community, and social capital (Hill et al., 2019). How are these gains made available to the communities outside the network membership? How could such a network not only study the development of effective teachers as future faculty but examine graduate education more holistically to include research competence alongside teaching skills development as discussed previously? Who would fund such an effort, especially if it were broadened beyond the STEM disciplines? Again, higher-level cooperation is necessary beyond even multi-institutional networks.

The Association of Graduate Schools (AGS) comprises graduate schools in Canada and the United States belonging to the Association of American Universities (AAU) and was a key shaper of graduate education in the North America in the early 1900s (Slate, 1994). It holds an annual conference and its members voluntarily participate to various degrees in the AAU Data Exchange (AAUDE) on graduate education–related topics. It has not participated in nor sponsored publicly disseminated graduate education research projects as an organization until recently. The PhD Education Initiative (Association of American Universities,

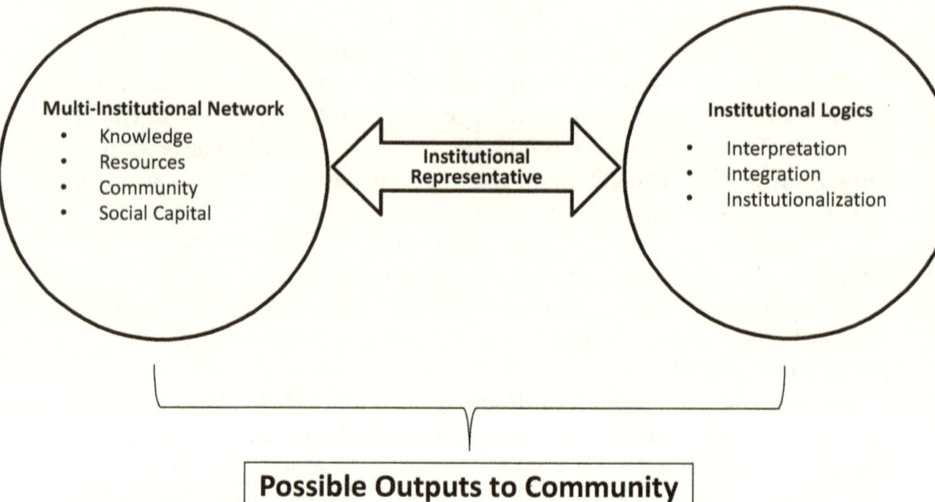

Figure 22. Modified multi-institutional network impact model. Adapted from Hill et al., 2019.

2020) is an effort to make doctoral education at AAU member institutions more student-centered with clearly visible pathways to a variety of careers. Exactly how this will be accomplished, who will have access to the results, and how applicable it will be to non-AAU member institutions remains to be seen. All AGS member institutions also belong to the Council of Graduate Schools (CGS), which is a larger member organization of graduate schools, primarily in Canada and the United States but with members around the world, whose mission is to promote graduate education and research through advocacy, research, and the dissemination of best practices. CGS conducts its own funded research, often in collaboration with other organizations; many of its publications have been cited in this monograph. Its mission limits how this work is carried out; that is, it primarily works with its members – graduate schools – and not directly with faculty, prospective students, degree-seeking students, advanced degree holders, or employers. There are certainly benefits to this approach, including improved participation rates, access to data, uniformity of questions on surveys, and a well-established mechanism for information dissemination; however, studies involving a larger set of institutions or aimed directly at prospective students, enrolled students, and advanced degree holders would likely have to be conducted through another mechanism.

In many countries around the world, that mechanism for research on advanced degree holders and graduate education at the national level comes through federal departments of education, their related research funding agencies, and international cooperation organizations. Representative works from the Research Councils UK, Deutsche Forschungsgemeinschaft, and Organisation for Economic Co-operation and Development, to name just a few, have been cited in this monograph. There are also international member organizations dedicated to graduate education beyond CGS. For example, even with some of its institutions participating in AGS and CGS, Canada has its own Canadian Association of Graduate Studies (CAGS). There are also international educational and scientific organizations that include graduate education as part of their portfolios, such as the American Association for the Advancement of Science (AAAS), European Association for International Education (EAIE), Institute of International Education (IIE), European University Association (EUA), Association of Public and Land-Grant Universities (APLU), and the Japan Society for the Promotion of Science (JSPS), among many others. They all should play a role in funding and carrying out foundational research on graduate education but their missions – hence, their research interests – are varied beyond the common interest in graduate education. International cooperation on research themes is the ideal but, in the end, the research projects that get funded have the most impact. The majority of funding decisions are made not by ministries of education or international member organizations but by research agencies and organizations.

Federal funding agencies have had perhaps the largest continuous influence on the shape and scope of research on graduate education. These agencies and some of the work they fund have been highlighted throughout this monograph. The amount of money they spend on graduate education research varies greatly by country, as does their disciplinary purview (e.g., science and engineering, or health sciences disciplines only), allowable funding (e.g., financial support for domestic students only), reporting structure and accountability, and requirements on dissemination of research findings. It is not the purpose of this monograph to describe the myriad variations that exist in research funding for graduate education around the world, nor even to suggest what might be optimal for the research topics laid out here. The funding mechanisms are what they are and time spent waiting for them to attain more favorable structures or political environments is time that could be better spent on initiating much-needed longitudinal studies. Researchers should do what they do best: propose sound research projects to the funding agencies. Funding agencies, in turn, should be clear on what type of research they value and what research will be of most benefit to the graduate education community. Their ability to positively influence graduate education through proposal and program requirements should not be underestimated or ignored.

Taken as a whole, there are no definitive answers to any of the organizational questions posed here, hence the justification for this monograph. Others have thought long and deeply about graduate education reform, exemplified by the following quote from one of the most relevant books on effecting change in doctoral [graduate] education in the United States:

> To be sure, change requires collective, cooperative action, and one encouraging attribute of the vision ... is that the same cast of characters moves from one role to another. The graduate students of the morning are the faculty and alumni of the afternoon. And the great majority of administrators, funders, and accreditors were once graduate students and faculty. So the perspectives, habits of mind, and opportunities to take leadership in service of improving [graduate] education are abundant and connected over time. (Walker et al., 2008)

The research agenda proposed here is not born from inactivity or indifference to pressing needs by those currently or formerly working in the graduate education research community. There are data and analyses on graduate education readily available, as there have been through the years. Recall, however, that over 50% of the current literature on graduate education comes from outside the United States. The articles cited here reflect the depth with which research on graduate education is conducted worldwide. The results from one institution in one country may not be applicable to graduate education around the world, but the questions are most certainly common and the information is sharable. The same type of routine information exchange that occurs through departmental and school seminars is rarely used to discuss innovations in graduate education. Instead, the graduate education community – at least in North America – relies heavily on expert reports (which often reside in the unindexed citation literature) that do not adequately contribute to this global knowledge base or rapid information dissemination. This heavy reliance on opinion as opposed to proof must change.

Emergent attempts to view graduate education in selected disciplines from a purely systems level approach may be premature (National Academies of Sciences, Engineering, and Medicine, 2018). At present, the system sensors are insufficiently sensitive and too thinly dispersed to provide the necessary input for such robust analysis. Perhaps the era of big data will improve the array of information-collection tools but, even then, the use of systems analysis to drive public policy decisions should be viewed with appropriate skepticism informed by experience (Hoos, 1972). Nevertheless, organizations such as the National Academies, AAAS, AGS, CAGS, and CGS, in proper coordination with funding agencies, professional societies, and international partners, can set the stage for regular, longitudinal research on graduate education at the macroscopic level. This effort will require more than collaboration on reports and recommendations. It will mean providing a framework and the necessary tools for sound, sustainable research such as regular, topical workshops; common databases; and guidelines for dissemination of information in the open literature. In this way, research can build upon itself and be of maximal benefit to its constituencies. Using the PhD program outcomes listed earlier as an example, could the graduate education community agree on at least a minimum set of standard program outcomes for the PhD, MFA, or any other graduate degree in the same way that the Accreditation Board for Engineering and Technology (ABET) (ABET, 2014) provides a minimum set of outcomes for all undergraduate engineering degree programs? It would certainly make assessment practices more standardized and provide a more uniform set of comparison criteria for prospective graduate students. The research literature that could flow from these comparative studies would be both voluminous and utilitarian.

As illustrated through the examples in this monograph, the current state of research on graduate education is insufficiently robust, especially given the level of federal, state, and private funding provided to students pursuing advanced degrees and the students' importance to global innovation and workforce development. It is perhaps ironic that the working hypothesis of the research agenda stated at the outset (there is as much [or more] to know and learn about graduate education as there is any other level of instruction) will provide the same benefits regardless of whether it is proved or disproved. The key is that it is tested. In either event, the scholars, administrators, artists, humanists, scientists, and educators comprising the graduate education enterprise will need to adopt the same commitment to quality scholarship to advance their industry that they used at one time to advance their individual careers.

References

Abeysekera, L., & Dawson, P. (2015). Motivation and cognitive load in the flipped classroom: Definition, rationale and a call for research. *Higher Education Research & Development, 34*(1), 1–14. https://doi.org/10.1080/07294360.2014.934336

Accreditation Board for Engineering and Technology (ABET). (2014). *Accreditation policy and procedure manual.* (No. A00 1 11/6/2014). Accreditation Board for Engineering and Technology. Retrieved from http://www.abet.org/wp-content/uploads/2015/05/A001-15-16-Accreditation-Policy-and-Procedure-Manual-03-19-151.pdf

Accreditation Council for Graduate Medical Education. (2017). *Common program requirements.* Retrieved from https://www.acgme.org/What-We-Do/Accreditation/Common-Program-Requirements

Acevedo-Gil, N., & Madrigal-Garcia, Y. (2018). Mentoring among Latina/o scholars: Enacting spiritual activism to navigate academia. *American Journal of Education, 124*(3), 313–44. https://doi.org/10.1086/697212

Ali, P.A., Watson, R., & Dhingra, K. (2016). Postgraduate research students' and their supervisors' attitudes towards supervision. *International Journal of Doctoral Studies,* (11), 227–41. https://doi.org/10.28945/3541

Allgood, S., Hoyt, G., & McGoldrick, K. (2018). The role of teaching and teacher training in the hiring and promotion of Ph.D. economists. *Southern Economic Journal, 84*(3), 912–27. https://doi.org/10.1002/soej.12252

Allison, R., & Ralston, M. (2018). Gender, anticipated family formation, and graduate school expectations among undergraduates. *Sociological Forum, 33*(1), 95–117. https://doi.org/10.1111/socf.12400

Allum, J.R., Kent, J.D.; & McCarthy, M.T. (2014). *Understanding PhD career pathways for program improvement.* Council of Graduate Schools.

American Academy of Arts and Sciences. (2015). *The state of the humanities: Higher education 2015.* American Academy of Arts and Sciences. Retrieved from https://www.amacad.org/publication/state-humanities-higher-education-2015

American Association for the Advancement of Science. (2016). *Professional ethics report: Archives.* Retrieved from http://www.aaas.org/page/professional-ethics-report-archives

American Chemical Society (ACS). (2013). *Advancing graduate education in the chemical sciences: Summary report of an ACS presidential commission.* Retrieved from http://www.acs.org/content/acs/en/about/governance/acs-presidential-commission-on-graduation-education-in-the-chemical-sciences.html

Andalib, M.A. (2019). Simulation of the leaky pipeline: Gender diversity in US K–graduate education. *Journal of Simulation,* https://doi.org/10.1080/17477778.2019.1620650

Appelt, S., van Beuzekom, B., Galindo-Rueda, F., & de Pinho, R. (2015). *Which factors influence the international mobility of research scientists?* Organisation for Economic Co-operation and Development. https://doi.org/10.1787/5js1tmrr2233-en

Arain, M., Haque, M., Johal, L., Mathur, P., Nel, W., Rais, A., Sandhu, R., & Sharma, S. (2013). Maturation of the adolescent brain. *Neuropsychiatric Disease and Treatment, 9,* 449–61. https://doi.org/10.2147/NDT.S39776

Arbeit, C.A., & Kang, K.H. (2017). *Field composition of postdocs shifts as numbers decline in biological sciences and in clinical medicine.* National Center for Science and Engineering Statistics.

Are graduate students worth keeping? (1970). *Nature, 225,* 985–6. https://doi.org/10.1038/225985a0

Ashby, M.T., & Maher, M.A. (2019). Consensus, division, and the future of graduate education in the chemical sciences. *Journal of Chemical Education, 96*(2), 196–202. https://doi.org/10.1021/acs.jchemed.8b00642

Association of American Medical Colleges. (2017). *Core competencies for entering medical students.* Retrieved from https://www.staging.aamc.org/initiatives/admissionsinitiative/competencies

Association of American Universities. (2020). *PhD education initiative.* Retrieved from https://www.aau.edu/education-community-impact/graduate-education/phd-education-initiative

Auriol, L., Misu, M., & Freeman, R.A. (2013). *Careers of doctorate holders.* Organisation for Economic Co-operation and Development. https://doi.org/10.1787/5k43nxgs289w-en

Auriol, L., Schaaper, M., & Felix, B. (2012). *Mapping careers and mobility of doctorate holders.* Organisation for Economic Co-operation and Development. https://doi.org/10.1787/5k4dnq2h4n5c-en

Austin, A.E. (2002). Preparing the next generation of faculty: Graduate school as socialization to the academic career. *The Journal of Higher Education, 73*(1), 94–122. https://doi.org/10.1080/00221546.2002.11777132

Austin, A.E., Campa, H., Pfund, C., Gillian-Daniel, D.L., Mathieu, R., & Stoddart, J. (2009). Preparing STEM doctoral students for future faculty careers. *New Directions for Teaching and Learning, 2009*(117), 83–95. https://doi.org/10.1002/tl.346

Baldwin, T., & Ford, J. (1988). Transfer of training: A review and directions for future research. *Personnel Psychology, 41*, 63–105. https://doi.org/10.1111/j.1744-6570.1988.tb00632.x

Baltes, B., Hoffman-Kipp, P., & Lynn, L. (2010). Students' research self-efficacy during online doctoral research courses. *Contemporary Issues in Education Research, 3*(3), 51. https://doi.org/10.19030/cier.v3i3.187

Bandura, A. (1997). *Self-efficacy: The exercise of control.* Macmillan.

Bartolone, J., Halverson, M.L., Hoffer, T.B., Wolniak, G.C., Setlak, L., Hedberg, E.C., Nielsen, E., Nhuan-Le, V., & Yisak, M. (2014). *Evaluation of the national science foundation's graduate research fellowship program: Final report.* (No. NSFDACS08D1596). NORC at the University of Chicago. Retrieved from http://www.nsf.gov/ehr/Pubs/GRFP_Final_Eval_Report_2014.pdf

Bauer, K.W., & Bennett, J.S. (2003). Alumni perceptions used to assess undergraduate research experience. *The Journal of Higher Education, 74*(2), 210–30. https://doi.org/10.1353/jhe.2003.0011

Becker, K.D. (2019). Graduate students' experiences of plagiarism by their professors. *Higher Education Quarterly, 73*(2), 251–65. https://doi.org/10.1111/hequ.12179

Belasco, A.S., Trivette, M.J., & Webber, K.L. (2014). Advanced degrees of debt: Analyzing the patterns and determinants of graduate student borrowing. *The Review of Higher Education, 37*(4), 469–97. https://doi.org/10.1353/rhe.2014.0030

Benbow, R., Byrd, D., & Connolly, M. (2011). *The Wisconsin Longitudinal Study of doctoral & postdoctoral teaching development key findings.* Retrieved from http://citeseerx.ist.psu.edu/viewdoc/download?doi=10.1.1.634.8444&rep=rep1&type=pdf.

Berdanier, C.G.P., Whitehair, C., Kirn, A., & Satterfield, D. (2020). Analysis of social media forums to elicit narratives of graduate engineering student attrition. *Journal of Engineering Education, 109*(1), 125–47. https://doi.org/10.1002/jee.20299

Berelson, B. (1960a). Conclusions, commentary, and recommendations. *Graduate education in the United States* (p. 233). McGraw-Hill.

Berelson, B. (1960b). *Graduate education in the United States.* McGraw-Hill.

Bernstein, M.J., Reifschneider, K., Bennett, I., & Wetmore, J.M. (2017). Science outside the lab: Helping graduate students in science and engineering understand the complexities of science policy. *Science and Engineering Ethics, 23*(3), 861–82. https://doi.org/10.1007/s11948-016-9818-6

Bersola, S.H., Stolzenberg, E.B., Love, J., & Fosnacht, K. (2014). Understanding admitted doctoral students' institutional choices: Student experiences versus faculty and staff perceptions. *American Journal of Education, 120,* 515–43. https://doi.org/10.1086/676923

Blessinger, P., & Stockley, D. (2016). *Emerging directions in doctoral education.* Emerald Group Publishing.

Blume, S., & Amsterdamska, O. (1987). *Post-graduate education in the 1980s.* Organisation for Economic Co-Operation and Development.

Blume-Kohout, M.E., & Adhikari, D. (2016). Training the scientific workforce: Does funding mechanism matter? *Research Policy, 45*(6), 1291–1303. https://doi.org/10.1016/j.respol.2016.03.011

Blume-Kohout, M.E., & Clack, J.W. (2013). Are graduate students rational? Evidence from the market for biomedical scientists. *PLoS One, 8*(12), e82759. https://doi.org/10.1371/journal.pone.0082759

Boden, D., Borrego, M., & Newswander, L.K. (2011). Student socialization in interdisciplinary doctoral education. *Higher Education, 62*(6), 741–55. https://doi.org/10.1007/s10734-011-9415-1

Bonwell, C.C., & Eison, J.A. (1991). Active learning: Creating excitement in the classroom. *1991 ASHE-ERIC higher education reports.* ERIC. Retrieved from https://eric.ed.gov/?q=).+Active+learning%3a+Creating+excitement+in+the+classroom.+1991+ASHE-ERIC+higher+education+reports&id=ED336049

Boote, D.N., & Beile, P. (2005). Scholars before researchers: On the centrality of the dissertation literature review in research preparation. *Educational Researcher, 34*(6), 3–15. https://doi.org/10.3102/0013189X034006003

Borrego, M., & Newswander, L.K. (2010). Definitions of interdisciplinary research: Toward graduate-level interdisciplinary learning outcomes. *The Review of Higher Education, 34*(1), 61–84. https://doi.org/10.1353/rhe.2010.0006

Bowen, W.G., & Rudenstine, N.L. (1992). *In pursuit of the PhD.* Princeton University Press.

Bowman, P.J. (2006). Role strain and adaptation issues in the strength-based model: Diversity, multilevel, and life-span considerations. *The Counseling Psychologist, 34*(1), 118–33. https://doi.org/10.1177/0011000005282374

Brailsford, I. (2010). Motives and aspirations for doctoral study: Career, personal, and inter-personal factors in the decision to embark on a history PhD. *International Journal of Doctoral Studies, 5,* 15–27. https://doi. org/10.28945/710

Brayboy, B.M.J., Castagno, A.E., & Solyom, J.A. (2014). Looking into the hearts of native peoples: Nation building as an institutional orientation for graduate education. *American Journal of Education, 120,* 575–96. https://doi.org/10.1086/676908

British Council. (2015). *The educational pathways of leaders: An international comparison.* Retrieved from https://www.britishcouncil.org/sites/default/files/edupathwaysofleadersreport_final.pdf

Britton, G. (2016). Bonfire of the humanities [Paper]. *Council of Graduate Schools Future of the Dissertation Workshop.* Retrieved from http://cgsnet.org/ckfinder/userfiles/files/1_2%20Britton.pdf

Brookhart, S.M. (1999). The art and science of classroom assessment. The missing part of pedagogy. *ASHE-ERIC Higher Education Report, 27*(1). ERIC. Retrieved from https://eric.ed.gov/?q=The+art+and+science+of+classroom+assessment.+The+missing+part+of+pedagogy&id=ED432938

Brown, J. (2010). *Literature review of research into attitudes towards electronic theses and dissertations (ETDs).* Retrieved from https://discovery.ucl.ac.uk/id/eprint/20424/1/20424.pdf

Bruce, A., Lyall, C., Tait, J., & Williams, R. (2004). Interdisciplinary integration in Europe: The case of the Fifth Framework Programme. *Futures, 36*(4), 457–70. https://doi.org/10.1016/j.futures.2003.10.003

Buizer, M., Ruthrof, K., Moore, S.A., Veneklaas, E.J., Hardy, G., & Baudains, C. (2015). A critical evaluation of interventions to progress transdisciplinary research. *Society & Natural Resources, 28*(6), 670–81. https://doi.org/10.1080/08941920.2014.945058

Burt, B.A., Knight, A., & Robeson, J. (2017). Racializing experiences of foreign-born and ethnically diverse Black male engineering graduate students: Implications for student affairs practice, policy, and research. *Journal of International Students,* 7(4), 925–43. https://doi.org/10.32674/jis.v7i4.182

Burt, B.A., Williams, K.L., & Palmer, G.J.M. (2019). It takes a village: The role of emic and etic adaptive strengths in the persistence of Black men in engineering graduate programs. *American Educational Research Journal, 56*(1), 39–74. https://doi.org/10.3102/0002831218789595

Burt, B.A., Williams, K.L., & Smith, W.A. (2018). Into the storm: Ecological and sociological impediments to Black males' persistence in engineering graduate programs. *American Educational Research Journal, 55*(5), 965–1006. https://doi.org/10.3102/0002831218763587

Canal-Domínguez, J.F., & Wall, A. (2014). Factors determining the career success of doctorate holders: Evidence from the Spanish case. *Studies in Higher Education, 39,* 1750–73. https://doi.org/10.1080/03075079.2013.806464

Cantor, J.A. (1997). *Experiential learning in higher education: Linking classroom and community.* ERIC. Retrieved from https://eric.ed.gov/?q=Experiential+learning+in+higher+education%3a+Linking+classroom+and+community&id=ED404948

Cantwell, B., Lee, J.J., & Mlambo, Y. (2018). International graduate student labor as mergers and acquisitions. *Journal of International Students, 8*(4), 1483–96. https://doi.org/10.32674/jis.v8i4.211

Carnevale, A.P., Rose, S.J., & Cheah, B. (2011). *The college payoff: Education, occupations, lifetime earnings.* ERIC. Retrieved from https://eric.ed.gov/?q=The+college+payoff&id=ED524299

Carraccio, C., Wolfsthal, S.D., Englander, R., Ferentz, K., & Martin, C. (2002). Shifting paradigms: From Flexner to competencies. *Academic Medicine, 77,* 361–7. https://doi.org/10.1097/00001888-200205000-00003

Cassuto, L. (2015). *The graduate school mess: What caused it and how we can fix it.* Harvard University Press.

Chea, T. (2013). Guy spent $11,000 on a coding "bootcamp" and doubled his salary. *Business Insider.* Retrieved from http://www.businessinsider.com/guy-spent-11000-on-a-coding-bootcamp-and-doubled-his-salary-2013-4

Chhinzer, N., & Russo, A.M. (2018). An exploration of employer perceptions of graduate student employability. *Education and Training, 60*(1), 104–20. https://doi.org/10.1108/ET-06-2016-0111

Christensen, G., Steinmetz, A., Alcorn, B., Bennett, A., Woods, D., & Emanuel, E.J. (2013). *The MOOC phenomenon: Who takes massive open online courses and why?* [Unpublished manuscript]. Retrieved April 5, 2016 from http://dx.doi.org/10.2139/ssrn.2350964

Clark, B.R. (1993). *The research foundations of graduate education: Germany, Britain, France, United States, Japan.* University of California Press.

Collaborative Institutional Training Initiative at the University of Miami. (2016). *Responsible conduct of research (RCR).* Retrieved from https://www.citiprogram.org/index.cfm?pageID=265

Colley, P., Schouten, K., Chabot, N., Downs, M., Anstey, L., Moulin, M.S., & Martin, R.E. (2019). Examining online health sciences graduate programs in Canada. *International Review of Research in Open and Distributed Learning, 20*(3), 255–67. https://doi.org/10.19173/irrodl.v20i4.4007

Columbaro, N.L. (2009). E-mentoring possibilities for online doctoral students: A literature review. *Adult Learning, 20*(3–4), 9–15. https://doi.org/10.1177/104515950902000305

Committee on Institutional Cooperation. (2016). *Universities: Measuring the impacts of research on innovation, competitiveness, and science.* Retrieved from https://www.btaa.org/docs/default-source/umetrics/umetrics-synthesis-document.pdf?sfvrsn=81f778f3_4

Committee on Maximizing the Potential of Women in Academic Science, Engineering (US), Committee on Science, & Public Policy (US). (2007). *Beyond bias and barriers: Fulfilling the potential of women in academic science and engineering.* National Academies Press.

Committee on Science, Engineering, and Public Policy. (1995). *Reshaping the graduate education of scientists and engineers.* National Academies Press. https://doi.org/10.17226/4935

Connolly, M.R., Savoy, J.N., Lee, Y., & Hill, L.B. (2016). *Building a better future STEM faculty: How doctoral teaching programs can improve undergraduate education.* Wisconsin Center for Education Research.

Council of Graduate Schools. (2004). *Ph.D. completion and attrition: Policy, numbers, leadership and next steps.* Council of Graduate Schools.

Council of Graduate Schools. (2013). *Completion and attrition in STEM master's programs.* Council of Graduate Schools.

Council of Graduate Schools. (2017). *The future of the doctoral dissertation.* Retrieved from http://cgsnet.org/future-doctoral-dissertation

Craig, C.J., Verma, R., Stokes, D., Evans, P., & Abrol, B. (2018). The influence of parents on undergraduate and graduate students' entering the STEM disciplines and STEM careers. *International Journal of Science Education, 40*(6), 621–43. https://doi.org/10.1080/09500693.2018.1431853

Crede, E., & Borrego, M. (2013). From ethnography to items: A mixed methods approach to developing a survey to examine graduate engineering student retention. *Journal of Mixed Methods Research, 7,* 62–80. https://doi.org/10.1177/1558689812451792

Crede, E., & Borrego, M. (2014). Understanding retention in US graduate programs by student nationality. *Studies in Higher Education, 39*(9), 1599–1616. https://doi.org/10.1080/03075079.2013.801425

Cummings, S.M., Chaffin, K.M., & Milam, A. (2019). Comparison of an online and a traditional MSSW program: A 5-year study. *Journal of Social Work Education, 55*(1), 176–87. https://doi.org/10.1080/10437797.2018.1508391

Cuthbert, D., & Molla, T. (2015). PhD crisis discourse: A critical approach to the framing of the problem and some Australian "solutions." *Higher Education, 69*(1), 33–53. https://doi.org/10.1007/s10734-014-9760-y

Czujko, R., & Anderson, G. (2015). *Common careers of physicists in the private sector: PhDs educated in the US 10–15 years earlier.* Statistical Research Center, American Institute of Physics. Retrieved from https://www.aip.org/sites/default/files/statistics/phd-plus-10/PhysPrivSect.pdf

Dabney, K.P., & Tai, R.H. (2014). Factors associated with female chemist doctoral career choice within the physical sciences. *Journal of Chemical Education, 91*(11), 1777–86. https://doi.org/10.1021/ed4008815

Dale, S.B., & Krueger, A.B. (2014). Estimating the effects of college characteristics over the career using administrative earnings data. *Journal of Human Resources, 49*(2), 323–58. https://doi.org/10.1353/jhr.2014.0015

Davis, M., & Feinerman, A. (2012). Assessing graduate student progress in engineering ethics. *Science and Engineering Ethics, 18,* 351–67. https://doi.org/10.1007/s11948-010-9250-2

Davis, O.C., & Nakamura, J. (2010). A proposed model for an optimal mentoring environment for medical residents: A literature review. *Academic*

Medicine: Journal of the Association of American Medical Colleges, 85(6), 1060–6. https://doi.org/10.1097/ACM.0b013e3181dc4aab

DeAngelo, L. (2010). Preparing for the PhD at a comprehensive institution: Perceptions of the "barriers." *Journal of the Professoriate*, 3(2), 17–49.

DeAngelo, L. (2016). *Supporting students of color on the pathway to graduate education.* (Data Brief No. 15-02). Council of Graduate Schools.

DeAngelo, L.T. (2008). *Increasing faculty diversity: How institutions matter to the PhD aspirations of undergraduate students* [Doctoral dissertation]. University of California, Los Angeles.

Denecke, D., Feaster, K., Okahana, H., Allum, J.R., & Stone, K. (2016). *Financial education: Developing high impact programs for graduate and undergraduate students.* Council of Graduate Schools.

Denecke, D., Feaster, K., & Stone, K. (2017). *Professional development: Shaping effective programs for STEM graduate students.* Council of Graduate Schools.

Department of Education. (2020). *Integrated postsecondary education data system.* Retrieved from https://nces.ed.gov/ipeds/use-the-data

Deutsche Forschungsgemeinschaft. (2020, February 13). *Excellence strategy.* Retrieved from https://www.dfg.de/en/research_funding/programmes/excellence_strategy/index.html

Diamond, A., Ball, C., Vorley, T., Hughes, T., Moreton, R., Howe, P., & Nathwani, T. (2014). *The impact of doctoral careers.* CFE Research.

Duckworth, A.L., Peterson, C., Matthews, M.D., & Kelly, D.R. (2007). Grit: Perseverance and passion for long-term goals. *Journal of Personality and Social Psychology, 92*, 1087–101. https://doi.org/10.1037/0022-3514.92.6.1087

Dunn, M.C., & Bourne, P.E. (2017). Building the biomedical data science workforce. *PLoS Biology, 15*(7), e2003082. https://doi.org/10.1371/journal.pbio.2003082

Eccles, J.S. (2005). Subjective task value and the Eccles et al. model of achievement-related choices. In A.J. Elliot & C.S. Dweck (Eds.), *Handbook of competence and motivation* (pp. 105–21). The Guilford Press.

Edminster, J., & Moxley, J. (2002). Graduate education and the evolving genre of electronic theses and dissertations. *Computers and Composition, 19*, 89–104. https://doi.org/10.1016/S8755-4615(02)00082-8

Ehrenberg, R.G., Jakubson, G.H., Groen, J.A., So, E., & Price, J. (2007). Inside the black box of doctoral education: What program characteristics influence doctoral students' attrition and graduation probabilities? *Educational Evaluation and Policy Analysis, 29*, 134–50. https://doi.org/10.3102/0162373707301707

Ehrenberg, R.G., & Mavros, P. (1995). Do doctoral students' financial support patterns affect their times-to-degree and completion probabilities? *Journal of Human Resources, 30*, 581–609. https://doi.org/10.2307/146036

Eide, E., Brewer, D., & Ehrenberg, R.G. (1998). Does it pay to attend an elite private college? Evidence on the effects of undergraduate college quality on graduate school attendance. *Economics of Education Review, 17*, 371–6. https://doi.org/10.1016/S0272-7757(97)00037-X

Eigenbrode, S.D., O'Rourke, M., Wulfhorst, J., Althoff, D.M., Goldberg, C.S., Merrill, K., Morse, W., Nielsen-Pincus, M., Stephens, J., Winowiecki, L., & Bosque-Pérez, N.A. (2007). Employing philosophical dialogue in collaborative science. *Bioscience, 57*(1), 55–64. https://doi.org/10.1641/B570109

Enders, J. (2004). Higher education, internationalisation, and the nation-state: Recent developments and challenges to governance theory. *Higher Education, 47*(3), 361–82. https://doi.org/10.1023/B:HIGH.0000016461.98676.30

Englander, R., Cameron, T., Ballard, A.J., Dodge, J., Bull, J., & Aschenbrener, C.A. (2013). Toward a common taxonomy of competency domains for the health professions and competencies for physicians. *Academic Medicine: Journal of the Association of American Medical Colleges, 88*(8), 1088–94. https://doi.org/10.1097/ACM.0b013e31829a3b2b

Epstein, R.M. (2007). Assessment in medical education. *The New England Journal of Medicine, 2007*(356), 387–96. https://doi.org/10.1056/NEJMra054784

Ermini, B., Papi, L., & Scaturro, F. (2017). An analysis of the determinants of over-education among Italian Ph.D graduates. *Italian Economic Journal, 3*(2), 167–207. https://doi.org/10.1007/s40797-017-0053-3

Espino, M.M. (2014). Exploring the role of community cultural wealth in graduate school access and persistence for Mexican American PhDs. *American Journal of Education, 120*, 545–74. https://doi.org/10.1086/676911

Evers, A., & Sieverding, M. (2015). Academic career intention beyond the PhD: Can the theory of planned behavior explain gender differences? *Journal of Applied Social Psychology, 45*(3), 158–72. https://doi.org/10.1111/jasp.12285

Feldon, D.F., Litson, K., Jeong, S., Blaney, J.M., Kang, J., Miller, C., Griffin, K., & Roksa, J. (2019). Postdocs' lab engagement predicts trajectories of PhD students' skill development. *Proceedings of the National Academy of Sciences of the United States of America, 116*(42), 20910–16. https://doi.org/10.1073/pnas.1912488116

Feldon, D.F., Maher, M.A., Hurst, M., & Timmerman, B. (2015). Faculty mentors', graduate students', and performance-based assessments of students' research skill development. *American Educational Research Journal, 52*, 334–70. https://doi.org/10.3102/0002831214549449

Feldon, D.F., Maher, M.A., Roksa, J., & Peugh, J. (2016). Cumulative advantage in the skill development of STEM graduate students: A mixed-methods study. *American Educational Research Journal, 53*(1), 132–61. https://doi.org/10.3102/0002831215619942

Feldon, D.F., Maher, M.A., & Timmerman, B.E. (2010). Performance-based data in the study of STEM Ph.D. education. *Science, 329*(5989), 282–3. https://doi.org/10.1126/science.1191269

Feldon, D.F., Peugh, J., Timmerman, B.E., Maher, M.A., Hurst, M., Strickland, D., Gilmore, J., & Stiegelmeyer, C. (2011). Graduate students' teaching experiences improve their methodological research skills. *Science, 333*(6045), 1037–9. https://doi.org/10.1126/science.1204109

Ferguson, K., Huang, B., Beckman, L., & Sinche, M. (2014). *National postdoctoral association institutional policy report 2014: Supporting and developing postdoctoral scholars.* National Postdoctoral Association.

Fisher, A.J., Mendoza-Denton, R., Patt, C., Young, I., Eppig, A., Garrell, R.L., Rees. D.C., Nelson, T.W., & Richards, M.A. (2019). Structure and belonging: Pathways to success for underrepresented minority and women PhD students in STEM fields. *PLoS One, 14*(1), e0209279. https://doi.org/10.1371/journal.pone.0209279

Fiske, S.J., Bennett, L.A., Ensworth, P., Redding, T., & Brondo, K. (2010). The changing face of anthropology: Anthropology masters reflect on education, careers, and professional organizations. *AAA/CoPAPIA 2009 Anthropology MA Career Survey.* American Anthropological Association. Retrieved from http://rdcms-aaa.s3.amazonaws.com/files/production/public/FileDownloads/pdfs/resources/researchers/upload/ChangingFaceofAnthropologyFinal.pdf

Fowler, J., & Muckert, T. (2004). Tiered mentoring: Engaging students with peers and professionals [Paper]. *Teaching and Learning Forum.* Griffith University. Retrieved from http://litec.curtin.edu.au/events/conferences/tlf/tlf2004/fowler-j.html

Fox, M. (1992). Student debt and enrollment in graduate and professional school. *Applied Economics, 24*(7), 669–77. https://doi.org/10.1080/00036849200000035

Frechtling, J. (2010). *The 2010 user-friendly handbook for project evaluation.* (No. 2010 revision to NSF 02-057). National Science Foundation. Retrieved from http://www.informalscience.org/sites/default/files/TheUserFriendlyGuide.pdf

Gaff, J.G. (2002). Preparing future faculty and doctoral education. *Change: The Magazine of Higher Learning, 34*(6), 63–6. https://doi.org/10.1080/00091380209605571

Gaff, J.G., Pruitt-Logan, A.S., Sims, L.B., & Denecke, D.D. (2003). *Preparing future faculty in the humanities and social sciences: A guide for change.* Council of Graduate Schools & Association of American Colleges and Universities.

Gale, K., Speedy, J., & Wyatt, J. (2010). Gatecrashing the oasis? A joint doctoral dissertation play. *Qualitative Inquiry, 16,* 21–8. https://doi.org/10.1177/1077800409349758

Galvez, S.M., Heiberger, R., & McFarland, D. (2019). Paradigm wars revisited: A cartography of graduate research in the field of education (1980–2010). *American Educational Research Journal.* https://doi.org/10.3102/0002831219860511

Gardner, S.K. (2009). The development of doctoral students: Phases of challenge and support. In *ASHE Higher Education Report, 34*(6). Wiley Subscription Services, Inc., A Wiley Company. https://doi.org/10.1002/aehe.3406

Gardner, S.K. (2013). The challenges of first-generation doctoral students. *New Directions for Higher Education, 2013*(163), 43–54. Retrieved from https://onlinelibrary.wiley.com/doi/abs/10.1002/he.20064

Gemme, B., & Gingras, Y. (2012). Academic careers for graduate students: A strong attractor in a changed environment. *Higher Education, 63*(6), 667–83. https://doi.org/10.1007/s10734-011-9466-3

Ghiasi, A., Fountas, G., Anastasopoulos, P., & Mannering, F. (2019). Statistical assessment of peer opinions in higher education rankings the case of US engineering graduate programs. *Journal of Applied Research in Higher Education, 11*(3), 481–92. https://doi.org/10.1108/JARHE-09-2018-0196

Gibbs Jr., K.D., McGready, J., Bennett, J.C., & Griffin, K. (2014). Biomedical science Ph.D. career interest patterns by race/ethnicity and gender. *PLoS One, 9*(12), e114736. https://doi.org/10.1371/journal.pone.0114736

Gibbs, K.D., Basson, J., Xierali, I.M., & Broniatowski, D.A. (2016). Decoupling of the minority PhD talent pool and assistant professor hiring in medical school basic science departments in the US. *eLife, 5.* https://doi.org/10.7554/eLife.21393

Gittings, G.A. (2010). The effect of student attributes and program characteristics on doctoral degree completion (Paper 502) [Doctoral dissertation, University of Louisville and Western Kentucky University]. ThinkIR. https://doi.org/10.18297/etd/502

Gittings, G., Bergman, M.J., & Osam, K. (2018). The doctoral quest: Managing variables that impact degree completion. *Faculty Scholarship,* 395. Retrieved from https://ir.library.louisville.edu/faculty/395

Gittings, G., Bergman, M., Shuck, B., & Rose, K. (2018). The impact of student attributes and program characteristics on doctoral degree completion. *New Horizons in Adult Education and Human Resource Development, 30*(3), 3–22. https://doi.org/10.1002/nha3.20220

Goff, S.A., Vaughn, M., McKay, S., Lyons, E., Stapleton, A.E., Gessler, D., Matasci, N., Wang, L., Hanlon, M., Lenards, A., Muir, A., Merchant, N., Lowry, S., Mock, S., Helmke, M., Kubach, A., Narro, M., Hopkins, N., Micklos, D., ... Stanzione, D. (2011). The iPlant collaborative: Cyberinfrastructure for plant biology. *Frontiers in Plant Science, 2.* https://doi.org/10.3389/fpls.2011.00034

Goldberg, A.E., Kuvalanka, K., & Dickey, L. (2019). Transgender graduate students' experiences in higher education: A mixed-methods exploratory study. *Journal of Diversity in Higher Education, 12*(1), 38–51. https://doi.org/10.1037/dhe0000074

Golde, C.M. (2007). Signature pedagogies in doctoral education: Are they adaptable for the preparation of education researchers? *Educational Researcher, 36*(6), 344–51. https://doi.org/10.3102/0013189X07308301

Golde, C.M., & Dore, T.M. (2001). *At cross purposes: What the experiences of today's doctoral students reveal about doctoral education.* ERIC. Retrieved from https://eric.ed.gov/?id-ED450628

Golde, C.M., & Gallagher, H.A. (1999). The challenges of conducting interdisciplinary research in traditional doctoral programs. *Ecosystems, 2*(4), 281–5. https://doi.org/10.1007/s100219900076

Goldsmith, S.G., Presley, J.B., & Cooley, E.A. (2002). *National science foundation graduate research fellowship program final evaluation report.* (No. nsf02080). National Science Foundation. Retrieved from www.nsf.gov/pubs/2002/nsf02080/nsf02080.pdf

González, R. (2019). *Graduate students of color: The impact of mentoring at predominantly white institutions* [Doctoral dissertation]. Colorado State University.

Gopaul, B. (2019). "Nothing succeeds like success": Doctoral education and cumulative advantage. *Review of Higher Education, 42*(4), 1431–57. https://doi.org/10.1353/rhe.2019.0071

Gornitzka, A., Kogan, M., & Amaral, A. (2005). *Reform and change in higher education. Analyzing policy implementation.* Springer.

Graddy-Reed, A., Lanahan, L., & Ross, N.M. (2016). The effect of R&D investment on graduate student productivity: Evidence from the life sciences [Paper]. *Association for Public Policy Analysis & Management 2016 Fall Research Conference.*

Graddy-Reed, A., Lanahan, L., & Ross, N.M. (2017). Influences of academic institutional factors on R&D funding for graduate students. *Science and Public Policy, 44*(6), 1–21. https://doi.org/10.1093/scipol/scx017

Graduate Assembly, The. (2014). *Graduate student happiness & well-being report, 2014.* University of California, Berkeley. Retrieved from http://ga.berkeley.edu/wellbeingreport

Grafton, A.T., & Grossman, J. (2011). No more plan B: A very modest proposal for graduate programs in history. *Perspectives on History, 49*(5)

Granello, D.H. (2001). Promoting cognitive complexity in graduate written work: Using Bloom's taxonomy as a pedagogical tool to improve literature reviews. *Counselor Education and Supervision, 40*(4), 292. https://doi.org/10.1002/j.1556-6978.2001.tb01261.x

Graybill, J.K., Dooling, S., Shandas, V., Withey, J., Greve, A., & Simon, G.L. (2006). A rough guide to interdisciplinarity: Graduate student perspectives. *Bioscience, 56*(9), 757–63. https://doi.org/10.1641/0006-3568(2006)56[757:ARGTIG]2.0.CO;2

Green, D., Pulley, T., Jackson, M., Martin, L.L., & Fasching-Varner, K.J. (2018). Mapping the margins and searching for higher ground: Examining the marginalisation of Black female graduate students at PWIs. *Gender and Education, 30*(3), 295–309. https://doi.org/10.1080/09540253.2016.1225009

Grindel, T. (2006). *In search of global engineering excellence.* Continental AG.

Groen, J.A., Jakubson, G.H., Ehrenberg, R.G., Condie, S., & Liu, A.Y. (2008). Program design and student outcomes in graduate education. *Economics of Education Review, 27*(2), 111–24. https://doi.org/10.1016/j.econedurev.2006.09.010

Guerin, C., Jayatilaka, A., & Ranasinghe, D. (2015). Why start a higher degree by research? An exploratory factor analysis of motivations to undertake doctoral studies. *Higher Education Research & Development, 34,* 89–104. https://doi.org/10.1080/07294360.2014.934663

Haak, L.L., Baker, D., Ginther, D.K., Gordon, G.J., Probus, M.A., Kannankutty, N., & Weinberg, B.A. (2012). Standards and infrastructure for innovation data exchange. *Science, 338,* 196–7. https://doi.org/10.1126/science.1221840

Hanks, A.S., & Kniffin, K.M. (2014). Early career PhD salaries: The industry premium and interdisciplinary debate. *Applied Economics Letters, 21,* 1277–82. https://doi.org/10.1080/13504851.2014.922664

Harman, K.M. (2004). Producing "industry-ready" doctorates: Australian Cooperative Research Centre approaches to doctoral education. *Studies in Continuing Education, 26*(3), 387–404. https://doi.org/10.1080/0158037042000265944

Hayter, C.S., Lubynsky, R., & Maroulis, S. (2017). Who is the academic entrepreneur? The role of graduate students in the development of university spinoffs. *Journal of Technology Transfer, 42*(6), 1237–54. https://doi.org/10.1007/s10961-016-9470-y

Heidler, R. (2015). *Drivers of internationalisation: Results from the evaluation of international research training groups.* Deutsche Forschungsgemeinschaft. Retrieved from http://www.dfg.de/download/pdf/dfg_im_profil/geschaeftsstelle/publikationen/infobriefe/ib02_2015en.pdf

Herzig, A. (2004). Becoming mathematicians: Women and students of color choosing and leaving doctoral mathematics. *Review of Educational Research, 74,* 171–214. https://doi.org/10.3102/00346543074002171

Hildt, E., Laas, K., Miller, C., Taylor, S., & Brey, E.M. (2019). Empowering graduate students to address ethics in research environments. *Cambridge Quarterly of Healthcare Ethics, 28*(3), 542–50. https://doi.org/10.1017/S096318011900046X

Hill, L.B., Savoy, J.N., Austin, A.E., & Bantawa, B. (2019). The impact of multi-institutional STEM reform networks on member institutions: A case study of CIRTL. *Innovative Higher Education, 44*(3), 187–202. https://doi.org/10.1007/s10755-019-9461-7

Hlaing, W.M. (2019). Competencies acquired in epidemiology doctoral programs. *Annals of Epidemiology, 36,* 1–4. https://doi.org/10.1016/j.annepidem.2019.06.005

Holbrook, A., Bourke, S., & Fairbairn, H. (2015). Examiner reference to theory in PhD theses. *Innovations in Education and Teaching International, 52,* 75–85. https://doi.org/10.1080/14703297.2014.981842

Hoos, I.R. (1972). *Systems analysis in social policy: A critical review.* University of California Press.

Hopwood, N. (2010). Doctoral experience and learning from a sociocultural perspective. *Studies in Higher Education, 35,* 829–43. https://doi.org/10.1080/03075070903348412

Hughes, C.C., Schilt, K., Gorman, B.K., & Bratter, J.L. (2017). Framing the faculty gender gap: A view from STEM doctoral students. *Gender Work and Organization, 24*(4), 398–416. https://doi.org/10.1111/gwao.12174

Hund, A.K., Churchill, A.C., Faist, A.M., Havrilla, C.A., Love Stowell, S.M., McCreery, H.F., Ng, J., Pinzone, C., & Scordato, E.S.C. (2018). Transforming mentorship in STEM by training scientists to be better leaders. *Ecology and Evolution, 8*(20), 9962–74. https://doi.org/10.1002/ece3.4527

Hyun, J.K., Quinn, B.C., Madon, T., & Lustig, S. (2006). Graduate student mental health: Needs assessment and utilization of counseling services. *Journal of College Student Development, 47*(3), 247–66. https://doi.org/10.1353/csd.2006.0030

Hyun, S.H. (2019). International graduate students in American higher education: Exploring academic and non-academic experiences of international graduate students in non-STEM fields. *International Journal of Educational Research, 96,* 56–62. https://doi.org/10.1016/j.ijer.2019.05.007

Jablonski, A.M. (2001). Doctoral studies as professional development of educators in the United States. *European Journal of Teacher Education, 24,* 215–21. https://doi.org/10.1080/02619760120095606

Jacobs, B., & van der Ploeg, F. (2006). Guide to reform of higher education: A European perspective. *Economic Policy, 21*(47), 536–92. https://doi.org/10.1111/j.1468-0327.2006.00166.x

Jaeger, A.J. (2003). Job competencies and the curriculum: An inquiry into emotional intelligence in graduate professional education. *Research in Higher Education, 44*(6), 615–39. https://doi.org/10.1023/A:1026119724265

Jennings Jr., E.T. (1989). Accountability, program quality, outcome assessment, and graduate education for public affairs and administration. *Public Administration Review, 49*(5), 438–46. https://doi.org/10.2307/976388

Julius, D.J., & Gumport, P.J. (2003). Graduate student unionization: Catalysts and consequences. *The Review of Higher Education, 26*(2), 187–216. https://doi.org/10.1353/rhe.2002.0033

Kaslow, N.J., Bangasser, D.A., Grus, C.L., McCutcheon, S.R., & Fowler, G.A. (2018). Facilitating pipeline progress from doctoral degree to first job. *American Psychologist, 73*(1), 47–62. https://doi.org/10.1037/amp0000120

Keck, A., Sloane, S., Liechty, J.M., Paceley, M.S., Donoyan, S.M., Bost, K.K., McBride, B.A., & Fiese, B.H. (2017). Longitudinal perspectives of faculty and students on benefits and barriers to transdisciplinary graduate education: Program assessment and institutional recommendations. *Palgrave Communications, 3,* 40. https://doi.org/10.1057/s41599-017-0027-y

Keefer, J.M., Wisker, G., & Kiley, M. (2015). Doctoral candidate learning. *Innovations in Education and Teaching International, 52,* 1–3. https://doi.org/10.1080/14703297.2015.983313

Kena, G., Hussar, W., McFarland, J., de Brey, C., Musu-Gillette, L., Wang, X., Zhang, J., Rathburn, A., Wilkinson-Flicker, S., Diliberti, M., Barmer, A., Bullock Mann, F., & Dunlop Velez, E. (2016). *The condition of education 2016.* (No. NCES 2016-144). National Center for Education Statistics. Retrieved from http://nces.ed.gov/pubsearch/pubsinfo.asp?pubid=2016144

Kena, G., Musu-Gillette, L., Robinson, J., Wang, X., Rathbun, A., Zhang, J., Wilkinson-Flicker, S., Barner, A., & Dunlop Velez, E. (2015). *The condition of education 2015.* (No. NCES 2015-144). National Center for Education Statistics. Retrieved from http://nces.ed.gov/pubsearch/pubsinfo.asp?pubid=2015144

Kent, J.D., & McCarthy, M.T. (2016). *Holistic review in graduate admissions.* Council of Graduate Schools.

Kirby, P.G., Biever, J.L., Martínez, I.G., & Gómez, J.P. (2004). Adults returning to school: The impact on family and work. *The Journal of Psychology, 138*(1), 65–76. https://doi.org/10.3200/JRLP.138.1.65-76

Kniffin, K.M., & Hanks, A.S. (2018). The trade-offs of teamwork among STEM doctoral graduates. *American Psychologist, 73*(4), 420–32. https://doi.org/10.1037/amp0000288

Knight, D., Kinoshita, T., Choe, N., & Borrego, M. (2018). Doctoral student funding portfolios across and within engineering, life sciences and physical sciences. *Studies in Graduate and Postdoctoral Education, 9*(1), 75–90. https://doi.org/10.1108/SGPE-D-17-00044

Kobayashi, S., Grout, B.W., & Rump, C.Ø. (2015). Opportunities to learn scientific thinking in joint doctoral supervision. *Innovations in Education and Teaching International, 52,* 41–51. https://doi.org/10.1080/14703297.2014.981837

Kogan, M., & Bauer, M. (2006). Higher education policies: Historical overview. *Transforming Higher Education,* 25–38. https://doi.org/10.1007/978-1-4020-4657-5_2

Kreth, Q., Spirou, M.E., Budenstein, S., & Melkers, J. (2019). How prior experience and self-efficacy shape graduate student perceptions of an online learning environment in computing. *Computer Science Education, 29*(4), 357–81. https://doi.org/10.1080/08993408.2019.1601459

Kyllonen, P., Walters, A.M., & Kaufman, J.C. (2005). Noncognitive constructs and their assessment in graduate education: A review. *Educational Assessment, 10*(3), 153–84. https://doi.org/10.1207/s15326977ea1003_2

Kyvik, S., & Olsen, T.B. (2014). Increasing completion rates in Norwegian doctoral training: Multiple causes for efficiency improvements. *Studies in Higher Education, 39*, 1668–82. https://doi.org/10.1080/03075079.2013.801427

Labour market: Bread lines for physicists. (1970). *Nature, 225*, 897–8. https://doi.org/10.1038/225897b0

Lafer, G. (2003). Graduate student unions: Organizing in a changed academic economy. *Labor Studies Journal, 28*(2), 25–43. https://doi.org/10.1177/0160449X0302800202

Larson, R.C., Ghaffarzadegan, N., & Xue, Y. (2014). Too many PhD graduates or too few academic job openings: The basic reproductive number R-0 in academia. *Systems Research and Behavioral Science, 31*, 745–50. https://doi.org/10.1002/sres.2210

Lawrence, K.A., Zentner, M., Wilkins-Diehr, N., Wernert, J.A., Pierce, M., Marru, S., & Michael, S. (2015). Science gateways today and tomorrow: Positive perspectives of nearly 5000 members of the research community. *Concurrency and Computation: Practice and Experience*, 4252–68. https://doi.org/10.1002/cpe.3526

Lawrence, N., Serdikoff, S., Zinn, T., & Baker, S. (2009). Have we demystified critical thinking? In D. Dun, J. Halonen, & R. Smith (Eds.), *Teaching critical thinking in psychology: A handbook of best practices* (pp. 22–33). Wiley-Blackwell.

LeCompte, M.D., Klingner, J.K., Campbell, S.A., & Menk, D.W. (2003). Editor's introduction. *Review of Educational Research, 73*(2), 123–4. https://doi.org/10.3102/00346543073002123

Lee, A. (2008). How are doctoral students supervised? Concepts of doctoral research supervision. *Studies in Higher Education, 33*(3), 267–81. https://doi.org/10.1080/03075070802049202

Lee, J.J., Oseguera, L., Kim, K.A., Fann, A., Davis, T.M., & Rhoads, R.A. (2004). Tangles in the tapestry: Cultural barriers to graduate student unionization. *The Journal of Higher Education, 75*(3), 340–61. https://doi.org/10.1080/00221546.2004.11772259

Lee, J.J., & Rice, C. (2007). Welcome to America? International student perceptions of discrimination. *Higher Education, 53*(3), 381–409. https://doi.org/10.1007/s10734-005-4508-3

Lee, L.M., McCarty, F.A., & Zhang, T.R. (2015). Ethical numbers: Ethics training in US graduate statistics programs, 2013–2014. *The American Statistician, 69*(1), 11–16. https://doi.org/10.1080/00031305.2014.997891

Lee, N., & Reithmeier, R. (2013). *A graduate course in professional development.* Retrieved from https://www.researchgate.net/profile/Nana_Lee2/publication/259472273_A_Graduate_Course_in_Professional_Development/links/00b7d52d5fc4289abc000000/A-Graduate-Course-in-Professional-Development.pdf

Lehker, T., & Furlong, J.S. (2006). Career services for graduate and professional students. *New Directions for Student Services, 2006*(115), 73–83. https://doi.org/10.1002/ss.217

Lent, R.W., Brown, S.D., & Hackett, G. (2002). Social cognitive career theory. *Career Choice and Development, 4,* 255–311.

Leshner, A.I., & Scherer, L. (2019). Critical steps toward modernizing graduate STEM education. *Issues in Science and Technology, 35*(2), 45–9.

Levecque, K., Anseel, F., De Beuckelaer, A., van der Heyden, J., & Gisle, L. (2017). Work organization and mental health problems in PhD students. *Research Policy, 46*(4), 868–79. https://doi.org/10.1016/j.respol.2017.02.008

Lewis, K.L., & Hodges, S.D. (2015). Expanding the concept of belonging in academic domains: Development and validation of the Ability Uncertainty Scale. *Learning and Individual Differences, 37,* 197–202. https://doi.org/10.1016/j.lindif.2014.12.002

Licastro, A., Davidson, C.N., Davis, J.E., Donovan, G.T., & Sousanis, N. (2016). *What is a dissertation? New models, methods, media.* Retrieved from http://mediacommons.org/alt-ac/pieces/beyond-proto-monograph-new-models-dissertation

Lim, S. (2003). The strangeness of creative writing: An institutional query. *Pedagogy, 3*(2), 151–69. https://doi.org/10.1215/15314200-3-2-151

Litalien, D., & Guay, F. (2015). Dropout intentions in PhD studies: A comprehensive model based on interpersonal relationships and motivational resources. *Contemporary Educational Psychology, 41,* 218–31. https://doi.org/10.1016/j.cedpsych.2015.03.004

Long, M.C. (2015). Is there a "workable" race-neutral alternative to affirmative action in college admissions? *Journal of Policy Analysis and Management, 34,* 162–83. https://doi.org/10.1002/pam.21800

Lopatto, D. (2007). Undergraduate research experiences support science career decisions and active learning. *CBE Life Sciences Education, 6*(4), 297–306. https://doi.org/10.1187/cbe.07-06-0039

Lubienski, S.T., Miller, E.K., & Saclarides, E.S. (2018). Sex differences in doctoral student publication rates. *Educational Researcher, 47*(1), 76–81. https://doi.org/10.3102/0013189X17738746

Lurie, S.J., Mooney, C.J., & Lyness, J.M. (2009). Measurement of the general competencies of the Accreditation Council for Graduate Medical Education: A systematic review. *Academic Medicine: Journal of the Association of*

American Medical Colleges, 84(3), 301–9. https://doi.org/10.1097/ACM.0b013e3181971f08

Malcom, L.E., & Dowd, A.C. (2012). The impact of undergraduate debt on the graduate school enrollment of STEM baccalaureates. *The Review of Higher Education, 35*(2), 265–305. https://doi.org/10.1353/rhe.2012.0007

Maltiel, R., Raftery, A.E., McCormick, T.H., & Baraff, A.J. (2015). Estimating population size using the network scale up method. *The Annals of Applied Statistics, 9*(3), 1247–77. https://doi.org/10.1214/15-AOAS827

Manathunga, C., & Lant, P. (2006). How do we ensure good PhD student outcomes? *Education for Chemical Engineers, 1*, 72–81. https://doi.org/10.1205/ece.05003

Martinez, A., Epstein, C., Parsad, A., & Whittaker, K. (2012). *Evaluation of the NSF's international research fellowship program: Final report.* Abt Associates. Retrieved from https://files.eric.ed.gov/fulltext/ED546146.pdf

Matusovich, H.M., Streveler, R.A., & Miller, R.L. (2010). Why do students choose engineering? A qualitative, longitudinal investigation of students' motivational values. *Journal of Engineering Education, 99*, 289–303. https://doi.org/10.1002/j.2168-9830.2010.tb01064.x

Mayhew, L.B. (1972). *Reform in graduate education.* Southern Regional Education Board.

Mayhew, L.B. (1980). *Graduate and professional education, 1980: A survey of institutional plans.* McGraw-Hill.

McAlpine, L., & Norton, J. (2006). Reframing our approach to doctoral programs: An integrative framework for action and research. *Higher Education Research & Development, 25*(1), 3–17. https://doi.org/10.1080/07294360500453012

McCarthy, M.T. (2016). Imagining the dissertation's many futures. *GradEdge, 5*(3), 1.

McCook, A. (2011). Rethinking PhDs. *Nature, 472*, 280–2. https://doi.org/10.1038/472280a

McCormick, T.H., Salganik, M.J., & Zheng, T. (2010). How many people do you know? Efficiently estimating personal network size. *Journal of the American Statistical Association, 105*(489), 59–70. https://doi.org/10.1198/jasa.2009.ap08518

McCormick, T.H., & Zheng, T. (2007). Adjusting for recall bias in "How many x's do you know?" surveys [Paper]. *Proceedings of the Joint Statistical Meetings.* Retrieved from http://www.stat.columbia.edu/~tzheng/files/McCormick_jsm07.pdf

Mearsheimer, J.J., & Walt, S.M. (2013). Leaving theory behind: Why simplistic hypothesis testing is bad for international relations. *European Journal of International Relations, 19*(3), 427–57. https://doi.org/10.1177/1354066113494320

Megginson, L. (2009). Noncognitive constructs in graduate admissions an integrative review of available instruments. *Nurse Educator, 34*, 254–61. https://doi.org/10.1097/NNE.0b013e3181bc7465

Mendenhall, R. (2012). What is competency-based education? *Huffington Post.* Retrieved from http://www.huffingtonpost.com/dr-robert-mendenhall/competency-based-learning-_b_1855374.html

Menzel, D.C. (1997). Teaching ethics and values in public administration: Are we making a difference? *Public Administration Review,* 224–30. https://doi.org/10.2307/976653

Merga, M.K., Mason, S., & Morris, J.E. (2019). "The constant rejections hurt": Skills and personal attributes needed to successfully complete a thesis by publication. *Learned Publishing, 32*(3), 271–81. https://doi.org/10.1002/leap.1245

Mille, N., & Brimicombe, A. (2004). Mapping research journeys across complex terrain with heavy baggage. *Studies in Continuing Education, 26*(3), 405–17. https://doi.org/10.1080/0158037042000265962

Miller, C., & Stassun, K. (2014). A test that fails. *Nature, 510*(7504), 303–4. https://doi.org/10.1038/nj7504-303a

Miller-Matero, L.R., Martinez, S., Maclean, L., Yaremchuk, K., & Ko, A.B. (2018). Grit: A predictor of medical student performance. *Education for Health, 31*(2), 109–13. https://doi.org/10.4103/efh.EfH_152_16

Millett, C.M. (2003). How undergraduate loan debt affects application and enrollment in graduate or first professional school. *Journal of Higher Education, 74*, 386–427. https://doi.org/10.1353/jhe.2003.0030

Millett, C.M., & Nettles, M.T. (2006). Expanding and cultivating the Hispanic STEM doctoral workforce: Research on doctoral student experiences. *Journal of Hispanic Higher Education, 5*, 258–87. https://doi.org/10.1177/1538192706287916

Miner, M.A. (2019). Unpacking the monolith intersecting gender and citizenship status in STEM graduate education. *International Journal of Sociology and Social Policy, 39*(9/10), 661–79. https://doi.org/10.1108/IJSSP-05-2019-0101

Mireles-Rios, R., & Garcia, N.M. (2019). What would your ideal graduate mentoring program look like? Latina/o student success in higher education. *Journal of Latinos and Education, 18*(4), 376–86. https://doi.org/10.1080/15348431.2018.1447937

Mirick, R.G., & Wladkowski, S.P. (2018). Pregnancy, motherhood, and academic career goals: Doctoral students' perspectives. *Affilia-Journal of Women and Social Work, 33*(2), 253–69. https://doi.org/10.1177/0886109917753835

Mitchell, B.S. (2019). Final report: Best practices in international research experiences for graduate students [Workshop] *2019 NSF Workshop.* Retrieved from http://nsfworkshop.wp.tulane.edu/wp-content/uploads/sites/378/2019/04/NSF-2019-Workshop-on-International-Research-Experiences-Final-Report.pdf

Mitchell, B.S., Vögler, M., & Nerad, M. (2016). *Evaluating international research experiences for graduate students.* Council of Graduate Schools. Retrieved from http://cgsnet.org/ckfinder/userfiles/files/CGS%20-%20Evaluating%20International%20Research%20Experiences%20-%20Final%20Report%20-%202016.pdf

Mokhtar, M. (2012). Intentions and expectations of female PhD students in engineering at one university in Malaysia. *Procedia – Social and Behavioral Sciences, 56,* 204–12. https://doi.org/10.1016/j.sbspro.2012.09.647

Moneta-Koehler, L., Brown, A.M., Petrie, K.A., Evans, B.J., & Chalkley, R. (2017). The limitations of the GRE in predicting success in biomedical graduate school. *PLoS One, 12*(1), e0166742. https://doi.org/10.1371/journal.pone.0166742

Montgomery, M., & Anderson, K. (2007). Best laid plans: Gender and the MBA completion rates of GMAT registrants. *The Quarterly Review of Economics and Finance, 47*(1), 175–91. https://doi.org/10.1016/j.qref.2005.08.005

Morley, L. (2014). Lost leaders: Women in the global academy. *Higher Education Research & Development, 33*(1), 114–28. https://doi.org/10.1080/07294360.2013.864611

Mullen, A.L., Goyette, K.A., & Soares, J.A. (2003). Who goes to graduate school? Social and academic correlates of educational continuation after college. *Sociology of Education,* 143–69. https://doi.org/10.2307/3090274

Nagy, G.A., Fang, C.M., Hish, A.J., Kelly, L., Nicchitta, C.V., Dzirasa, K., & Rosenthal, M.Z. (2019). Burnout and mental health problems in biomedical doctoral students. *CBE-Life Sciences Education, 18*(2). https://doi.org/10.1187/cbe.18-09-0198

National Academies of Sciences, Engineering, and Medicine. (2014). *The postdoctoral experience revisited.* National Academies Press. Retrieved from https://www.nae.edu/126985.aspx

National Academies of Sciences, Engineering, and Medicine. (2016). In Joe Alper (Ed.), *Developing a national STEM workforce strategy: A workshop summary.* National Academies Press. https://doi.org/10.17226/21900

National Academies of Sciences, Engineering, and Medicine. (2017a). *Supporting students' college success: The role of assessment of intrapersonal and interpersonal competencies.* National Academies Press. https://doi.org/10.17226/24697

National Academies of Sciences, Engineering, and Medicine. (2017b). *Fostering integrity in research.* National Academies Press.

National Academies of Sciences, Engineering, and Medicine. (2018). *Graduate STEM education for the 21st century.* National Academies Press.

National Academy of Engineering. (2016). *Grand challenges for engineering: Imperatives, prospects, and priorities.* National Academies Press. https://doi.org/10.17226/23440

National Center for Science and Engineering Statistics. (2017a). *Doctorate recipients from US universities 2015.* (Special Report No. NSF 15-306). National Science Foundation. Retrieved from https://www.nsf.gov/statistics/2017/nsf17306/static/report/nsf17306.pdf

National Center for Science and Engineering Statistics. (2017b). *NSF survey of earned doctorates 2015 – table 35.* National Science Foundation. Retrieved from https://www.nsf.gov/statistics/2017/nsf17306/data/tab35.pdf

National Center for Science and Engineering Statistics. (2019a). *Doctorate recipients from US universities 2018.* National Science Foundation. Retrieved from https://ncses.nsf.gov/pubs/nsf20301/downloads

National Center for Science and Engineering Statistics. (2019b). *Doctorate recipients from US universities 2018 data tables and resources, table 12.* (No. NSF 20-301). National Science Foundation. Retrieved from https://ncses.nsf.gov/pubs/nsf20301/downloads

National Institutes of Health. (2009). *Update on the requirement for instruction in the responsible conduct of research.* Retrieved from https://grants.nih.gov/grants/guide/notice-files/NOT-OD-10-019.html

National Institutes of Health. (2012). *Biomedical research workforce working group report.* National Institutes of Health. Retrieved from https://acd.od.nih.gov/documents/reports/Biomedical_research_wgreport.pdf

National Institutes of Health. (2014). *Revised policy: Descriptions on the use of individual development plans (IDPs) for graduate students and postdoctoral researchers required in annual progress reports beginning October 1, 2014.* Retrieved from http://grants.nih.gov/grants/guide/notice-files/NOT-OD-14-113.html

National Postdoctoral Association. (2017). *Postdoctoral teaching fellowships.* Retrieved from http://www.nationalpostdoc.org/?page=TeachingFellowships

National Research Council. (2005). *Policy implications of international graduate students and postdoctoral scholars in the United States.* National Academies Press. https://doi.org/10.17226/11289

National Research Council. (2010). *Research at the intersection of the physical and life sciences.* National Academies Press.

National Research Council. (2014a). *Convergence: Facilitating transdisciplinary integration of life sciences, physical sciences, engineering, and beyond.* National Academies Press.

National Research Council. (2014b). *Developing assessments for the next generation science standards.* National Academies Press. Retrieved from http://www.nap.edu/catalog/18409/developing-assessments-for-the-next-generation-science-standards

National Science and Technology Council. (2013). *Federal science, technology, engineering, and mathematics (STEM) education: 5-year strategic plan.* Committee on STEM Education National Science and Technology Council. Retrieved from https://www.whitehouse.gov/sites/default/files/microsites/ostp/stem_stratplan_2013.pdf

National Science Board. (2015). *Revisiting the STEM workforce, A companion to science and engineering indicators 2014.* (No. NSB-2015-10). National Science Foundation.

National Science Foundation. (2015). *Grant proposal guide.* Retrieved from http://www.nsf.gov/pubs/policydocs/pappguide/nsf15001/gpg_2.jsp#IIC2j

Nerad, M. (2012). Conceptual approaches to doctoral education: A community of practice. *Alternation, 19*(2), 57–72.

Nerad, M., June, R., & Miller, D.S. (1997). *Graduate education in the United States.* Routledge.

Newswander, L., & Borrego, M. (2009). Using journal clubs to cultivate a community of practice at the graduate level. *European Journal of Engineering Education, 34*(6), 561–71. https://doi.org/10.1080/03043790903202959

Nielsen-Pincus, M., Morse, W.C., Force, J.E., & Wulfhorst, J. (2007). Bridges and barriers to developing and conducting interdisciplinary graduate-student team research. *Ecology & Society, 12*(2), 8. Retrieved from http://www.ecologyandsociety.org/vol12/iss2/art8/

Noble, K.A. (1994). *Changing doctoral degrees: An international perspective.* The Society for Research into Higher Education.

NSF Survey of Earned Doctorates/Doctorate Records File. (2017). *NSF survey of earned doctorates/doctorate records file.* Retrieved from https://ncsesdata.nsf.gov/webcaspar/index.jsp?subHeader=WebCASPARHome

OECD Publishing. (2010). *The OECD innovation strategy: Getting a head start on tomorrow.* OECD Publishing.

Okahana, H. (2019). *Closing gaps in our knowledge of PhD career pathways: Job changes of PhD graduates after earning their degree* [Research brief]. Council of Graduate Schools.

Okahana, H., Feaster, K., & Allum, J. (2016). *Graduate enrollment and degrees: 2005 to 2015.* Council of Graduate Schools.

Okahana, H., & Hao, Y. (2019). Are they worth it? Master's degrees and labor market outcomes in the STEM workforce. *Innovative Higher Education, 44*(3), 165–85. https://doi.org/10.1007/s10755-019-9455-5

Okahana, H., & Kinoshita, T. (2018). *Closing gaps in our knowledge of PhD career pathways: Preparing future faculty for all types of colleges and universities* [Research brief]. Council of Graduate Schools.

Okuda, T., & Anderson, T. (2018). Second language graduate students' experiences at the writing center: A language socialization perspective. *Tesol Quarterly, 52*(2), 391–413. https://doi.org/10.1002/tesq.406

Oregon State University. (2016). *Graduate program assessment at OSU.* Retrieved from http://gradschool.oregonstate.edu/faculty/program-assessment

Ostriker, J.P., Kuh, C.V., & Voytuk, J.A. (2011). *A data-based assessment of research-doctorate programs in the United States.* National Academies Press.

Owens, J., & Lilly, F. (2017). The influence of academic discipline, race, and gender on web-use skills among graduate-level students. *Journal of Computing in Higher Education, 29*(2), 286–308. https://doi.org/10.1007/s12528-017-9137-1

Pacheco, W.I., Noel, R.J., Jr, Porter, J.T., & Appleyard, C.B. (2015). Beyond the GRE: Using a composite score to predict the success of Puerto Rican students in a biomedical PhD program. *CBE Life Sciences Education, 14*(2). https://doi.org/10.1187/cbe.14-11-0216

Park, H., Berkowitz, O., Symes, K., & Dasgupta, S. (2018). The art and science of selecting graduate students in the biomedical sciences: Performance in doctoral study of the foundational sciences. *PLoS One, 13*(4), e0193901. https://doi.org/10.1371/journal.pone.0193901

Patzer, B., Lazzara, E.H., Keebler, J.R., Madi, M.H., Dwyer, P., Huckstadt, A.A., & Smith-Campbell, B. (2017). Predictors of nursing graduate school success. *Nursing Education Perspectives, 38*(5), 272–4. https://doi.org/10.1097/01.NEP.0000000000000172

Pearson, M., & Kayrooz, C. (2004). Enabling critical reflection on research supervisory practice. *International Journal for Academic Development, 9*(1), 99–116. https://doi.org/10.1080/1360144042000296107

Pellegrino, J.W., & Hilton, M.L. (2013). *Education for life and work: Developing transferable knowledge and skills in the 21st century.* National Academies Press.

Perna, L.W. (2004). Understanding the decision to enroll in graduate school: Sex and racial/ethnic group differences. *The Journal of Higher Education, 75*(5), 487–527. https://doi.org/10.1353/jhe.2004.0032

Peters, D.L., & Daly, S.R. (2013). Returning to graduate school: Expectations of success, values of the degree, and managing the costs. *Journal of Engineering Education, 102*(2), 244–68. https://doi.org/10.1002/jee.20012

Petersen, S.L., Erenrich, E.S., Levine, D.L., Vigoreaux, J., & Gile, K. (2018). Multi-institutional study of GRE scores as predictors of STEM PhD degree completion: GRE gets a low mark. *PLoS One, 13*(10), e0206570. https://doi.org/10.1371/journal.pone.0206570

Pettigrew, A.M. (1990). Longitudinal field research on change: Theory and practice. *Organization Science, 1,* 267–92. https://doi.org/10.1287/orsc.1.3.267

Pezzoni, M., Mairesse, J., Stephan, P., & Lane, J. (2016). Gender and the publication output of graduate students: A case study. *PLoS One, 11,* e0145146. https://doi.org/10.1371/journal.pone.0145146

Pfund, C., House, S., Spencer, K., Asquith, P., Carney, P., Masters, K.S., McGee, R., Shanedling, J., Vecchiarelli, S., & Fleming, M. (2013). A research mentor training curriculum for clinical and translational researchers. *CTS–Clinical and Translational Science, 6,* 26–33. https://doi.org/10.1111/cts.12009

Pickett, C.L., Corb, B.W., Matthews, C.R., Sundquist, W.I., & Berg, J.M. (2015). Toward a sustainable biomedical research enterprise: Finding consensus and implementing recommendations. *Proceedings of the National Academy of Sciences.* https://doi.org/10.1073/pnas.1509901112

Porter, K.B., Posselt, J.R., Reyes, K., Slay, K.E., & Kamimura, A. (2018). Burdens and benefits of diversity work: Emotion management in STEM doctoral students. *Studies in Graduate and Postdoctoral Education, 9*(2), 127–43. https://doi.org/10.1108/SGPE-D-17-00041

Posselt, J. (2016). *Inside graduate admissions: Merit, diversity, and faculty gatekeeping.* Harvard University Press.

Posselt, J., Porter, K.B., & Kamimura, A. (2018). Organizational pathways toward gender equity in doctoral education: Chemistry and civil engineering compared. *American Journal of Education, 124*(4), 383–410. https://doi.org/10.1086/698457

Posselt, J., Reyes, K.A., Slay, K.E., Kamimura, A., & Porter, K.B. (2017). Equity efforts as boundary work: How symbolic and social boundaries shape access and inclusion in graduate education. *Teachers College Record, 119*(10), 100307.

Posselt, J.R. (2014). Toward inclusive excellence in graduate education: Constructing merit and diversity in PhD admissions. *American Journal of Education, 120,* 481–514. https://doi.org/10.1086/676910

Powell, R.R., Baker, L.M., & Mika, J.J. (2002). Library and information science practitioners and research. *Library & Information Science Research, 24*(1), 49–72. https://doi.org/10.1016/S0740-8188(01)00104-9

Prevost, L.B., Vergara, C.E., Urban-Lurain, M., & Campa, H.I. (2018). Evaluation of a high-engagement teaching program for STEM graduate students: Outcomes of the future academic scholars in teaching (FAST) fellowship program. *Innovative Higher Education, 43*(1), 41–55. https://doi.org/10.1007/s10755-017-9407-x

Prince, M. (2004). Does active learning work? A review of the research. *Journal of Engineering Education, 93*(3), 223–31. https://doi.org/10.1002/j.2168-9830.2004.tb00809.x

Pyne, J., & Grodsky, E. (2020). Inequality and opportunity in a perfect storm of graduate student debt. *Sociology of Education, 93*(1), 20–39. https://doi.org/10.1177/0038040719876245

Rasheem, S., Alleman, A., Mushonga, D., Anderson, D., & Vakalahi, H.F.O. (2018). Mentor-shape: Exploring the mentoring relationships of Black women in doctoral programs. *Mentoring & Tutoring, 26*(1), 50–69. https://doi.org/10.1080/13611267.2018.1445443

Regets, M.C. (2001). *Research and policy issues in high-skilled international migration: A perspective with data from the United States.* IZA Discussion paper series, No. 366

Reithmeier, R., O'Leary, L., Zhu, X., Dales, C., Abdulkarim, A., Aquil, A., Brouillard, L., Chang, S., Miller, S., Shi, W., Vu, N., & Zou, C. (2019).

The 10,000 PhDs project at the University of Toronto: Using employment outcome data to inform graduate education. *PLoS One, 14*(1), e0209898. https://doi.org/10.1371/journal.pone.0209898

Rice, K.G., Choi, C., Zhang, Y., Villegas, J., Ye, H.J., Anderson, D., Nesic, A., & Bigler, M. (2009). International student perspectives on graduate advising relationships. *Journal of Counseling Psychology, 56*(3), 376. https://doi.org/10.1037/a0015905

Ritter, K. (2001). Professional writers/writing professionals: Revamping teacher training in creative writing Ph.D. programs. *College English, 64*(2), 205–27. https://doi.org/10.2307/1350117

Rizzolo, S., DeForest, A.R., DeCino, D.A., Strear, M., & Landram, S. (2016). Graduate student perceptions and experiences of professional development activities. *Journal of Career Development, 43*(3), 195–210. https://doi.org/10.1177/0894845315587967

Roach, M., & Sauermann, H. (2010). A taste for science? PhD scientists' academic orientation and self-selection into research careers in industry. *Research Policy, 39*, 422–34. https://doi.org/10.1016/j.respol.2010.01.004

Roach, M., & Sauermann, H. (2017). The declining interest in an academic career. *PLoS One, 12*(9), e0184130. https://doi.org/10.1371/journal.pone.0184130

Robertson, J., & Bond, C. (2005). The research/teaching relation: A view from the edge. *Higher Education, 50*(3), 509–35. https://doi.org/10.1007/s10734-004-6365-x

Robertson, K.F., Smeets, S., Lubinski, D., & Benbow, C.P. (2010). Beyond the threshold hypothesis: Even among the gifted and top math/science graduate students, cognitive abilities, vocational interests, and lifestyle preferences matter for career choice, performance, and persistence. *Current Directions in Psychological Science, 19*, 346–51. https://doi.org/10.1177/0963721410391442

Rouse, W.B., Lombardi, J.V., & Craig, D.D. (2018). Modeling research universities: Predicting probable futures of public vs. private and large vs. small research universities. *Proceedings of the National Academy of Sciences of the United States of America, 115*(50), 12582–9. https://doi.org/10.1073/pnas.1807174115

Rubio, D.M., Primack, B.A., Switzer, G.E., Bryce, C.L., Seltzer, D.L., & Kapoor, W.N. (2011). A comprehensive career-success model for physician-scientists. *Academic Medicine, 86*, 1571–6. https://doi.org/10.1097/ACM.0b013e31823592fd

SACSCOC. (2017). *The principles of accreditation: Foundations for quality enhancement.* Southern Association of Colleges and Schools Commission on Colleges. Retrieved from https://sacscoc.org/app/uploads/2019/08/2018PrinciplesOfAcreditation.pdf

Salazar-Marquez, R. (2017). Digital immigrants in distance education. *International Review of Research in Open and Distributed Learning, 18*(6), 231–42. https://doi.org/10.19173/irrodl.v18i6.2967

Sargent, J.F. (2014). *The US science and engineering workforce: Recent, current, and projected employment, wages, and unemployment.* (No. R43061). Congressional Research Service.

Sauermann, H., & Roach, M. (2012). Science PhD career preferences: Levels, changes, and advisor encouragement. *PLoS One, 7*, e36307. https://doi.org/10.1371/journal.pone.0036307

Sauermann, H., & Roach, M. (2016). Scientific workforce. Why pursue the postdoc path? *Science, 352*(6286), 663–4. https://doi.org/10.1126/science.aaf2061

Schmaling, K.B., & Blume, A.W. (2009). Ethics instruction increases graduate students' responsible conduct of research knowledge but not moral reasoning. *Accountability in Research, 16*(5), 268–83. https://doi.org/10.1080/08989620903190323

Schmidt, A.H., Robbins, A.S.T., Combs, J.K., Freeburg, A., Jesperson, R.G., Rogers, H.S., Sheldon, K.S., & Wheat, E. (2012). A new model for training graduate students to conduct interdisciplinary, interorganizational and international research. *Bioscience, 62*(3), 296–304. https://doi.org/10.1525/bio.2012.62.3.11

Schöpfel, J., & Prost, H. (2013). Degrees of secrecy in an open environment: The case of electronic theses and dissertations. *ESSACHESS–Journal for Communication Studies, 6*(2(12)), 66–85. Retrieved from https://archivesic.ccsd.cnrs.fr/sic_01077239

Schrag, Z.M. (2011). The case against ethics review in the social sciences. *Research Ethics*, 7(4), 120–31. https://doi.org/10.1177/174701611100700402

Schwen, T.M., & Sorcinelli, M.D. (1983). A profile of a postdoctoral teaching program. *New Directions for Teaching and Learning, 1983*(15), 81–94. https://doi.org/10.1002/tl.37219831510

Shen, Y., & Herr, E.L. (2004). Career placement concerns of international graduate students: A qualitative study. *Journal of Career Development, 31*(1), 15–29. https://doi.org/10.1177/089484530403100102

Shin, J.C., Postiglione, G.A., & Ho, K.C. (2018). Challenges for doctoral education in East Asia: A global and comparative perspective. *Asia Pacific Education Review, 19*(2), 141–55. https://doi.org/10.1007/s12564-018-9527-8

Shin, J.C., Toutkoushian, R.K., & Teichler, U. (2011). *University rankings: Theoretical basis, methodology and impacts on global higher education.* Springer Science & Business Media.

Shortlidge, E.E., & Eddy, S.L. (2018). The trade-off between graduate student research and teaching: A myth? *PLoS One, 13*(6), e0199576. https://doi.org/10.1371/journal.pone.0199576

Shulman, L.S. (2005). Signature pedagogies in the professions. *Daedalus, 134*(3), 52–9. https://doi.org/10.1162/0011526054622015

Shumba, R., Ferguson-Boucher, K., Sweedyk, E., Taylor, C., Franklin, G., Turner, C., Sande, C., Acholonu, G., Bace, R., & Hall, L. (2013). Cybersecurity, women and minorities: Findings and recommendations from a preliminary investigation [Paper]. *Proceedings of the ITiCSE Working Group Reports Conference on Innovation and Technology in Computer Science Education–Working Group Reports,* 1–14.

Sisk, R.J. (2011). Team-based learning: Systematic research review. *Journal of Nursing Education, 50*(12), 665–9. https://doi.org/10.3928/01484834-20111017-01

Slantcheva-Durst, S., & Danowski, J. (2018). Effects of short-term international study trips on graduate students in higher education. *Journal of Student Affairs Research and Practice, 55*(2), 210–24. https://doi.org/10.1080/19496591.2018.1421203

Slate, A.N. (1994). *AGS: A history.* Association of Graduate Schools in the Association of American Universities.

Small, M. (2006). A case for including business ethics and the humanities in management programs. *Journal of Business Ethics, 64*(2), 195–211. https://doi.org/10.1007/s10551-005-5070-8

Snyder, T.D., de Brey, C., & Dillow, S.A. (2016). *Digest of education statistics, 2015.* (No. NCES 2016014). National Center for Educational Statistics. Retrieved from https://nces.ed.gov/pubsearch/pubsinfo.asp?pubid=2016014

Soares, L. (2012). *A "disruptive" look at competency-based education.* Retrieved from https://www.americanprogress.org/issues/higher-education/report/2012/06/07/11680/a-disruptive-look-at-competency-based-education/

Sorcinelli, M.D., Yun, J., & Baldi, B. (2016). *Mutual mentoring guide.* The Institute for Teaching Excellence & Faculty Development, University of Massachusetts. Retrieved from https://senate.ucsc.edu/committees/cca-committee-on-career-advising/faculty-career-resources/10.-mutual-network-mentoring-guide,-university-of-massachusetts,-amherst.pdf

Sosu, E.M. (2013). The development and psychometric validation of a Critical Thinking Disposition Scale. *Thinking Skills and Creativity, 9,* 107–19. https://doi.org/10.1016/j.tsc.2012.09.002

Southern Association of Colleges and Schools Commission on Colleges. (2018). *Faculty credentials – guidelines.* Retrieved from http://sacscoc.org/app/uploads/2019/07/faculty-credentials.pdf

Sowell, R., Allum, J., & Okahana, H. (2015). *Doctoral initiative on minority attrition and completion.* Council of Graduate Schools.

Sowell, R., Zhang, T., Bell, N., & Redd, K. (2008). *Ph.D. completion and attrition: Analysis of baseline demographic data from the ph.D. completion project.* Council of Graduate Schools.

Sowell, R., Zhang, T., & Redd, K. (2008). *Ph.D. completion and attrition: Analysis of baseline program data from the Ph.D. completion project.* Council of Graduate Schools.

Sowell, R.S., Bell, N.E., & Kirby, S.N. (2010). *Ph.D. completion and attrition: Policies and practices to promote student success.* Council of Graduate Schools.

Sowell, R.S., Bell, N.E., Kirby, S.N., & Naftel, S. (2009). *Ph.D. completion and attrition: Findings from exit survey of PhD completes.* Council of Graduate Schools.

Stanford University. (2016). *The individual development plan process.* Retrieved from https://biosciences.stanford.edu/current-students/idp/process/

Stein, S., Andreotti, V., & Boxall, R. (2019). The ethics of private funding for graduate students in the social sciences, arts, and humanities. *Critical Education, 10*(16), 1–17. https://doi.org/10.14288/ce.v10i16.186429

Sullivan, R.S., Dubnicki, A., & Dutkowsky, D.H. (2018). Research, teaching, and "other": What determines job placement of economics Ph.D.s? *Applied Economics, 50*(32), 3477–92. https://doi.org/10.1080/00036846.2018.1430331

Tarabochia, S., & Madden, S. (2018). In transition: Researching the writing development of doctoral students and faculty. *Writing & Pedagogy, 10*(3), 423–52. https://doi.org/10.1558/wap.34576

Taylor, M.C. (2011). Reform the PhD system or close it down. *Nature, 472,* 261. https://doi.org/10.1038/472261a

ten Have, H., & Ang, T.W. (2007). Unesco's global ethics observatory. *Journal of Medical Ethics, 33*(1), 15–16. https://doi.org/10.1136/jme.2006.016600

Thune, T. (2009). Doctoral students on the university–industry interface: A review of the literature. *Higher Education, 58*(5), 637. https://doi.org/10.1007/s10734-009-9214-0

Tierney, W.G. (1988). Organizational culture in higher education: Defining the essentials. *The Journal of Higher Education, 59*(1), 2–21. https://doi.org/10.1080/00221546.1988.11778301

Tinto, V. (1994). Toward a theory of doctoral persistence. In *Leaving college: Rethinking the causes and cures of student attrition* (pp. 230–56). University of Chicago Press. https://doi.org/10.7208/chicago/9780226922461.001.0001

Tractenberg, R.E., & FitzGerald, K.T. (2012). A mastery rubric for the design and evaluation of an institutional curriculum in the responsible conduct of research. *Assessment & Evaluation in Higher Education, 37*(8), 1003–21. https://doi.org/10.1080/02602938.2011.596923

Tregellas, J.R., Smucny, J., Rojas, D.C., & Legget, K.T. (2018). Predicting academic career outcomes by predoctoral publication record. *Peerj, 6,* e5707. https://doi.org/10.7717/peerj.5707

Truschke, A. (2015, April 6). *Open access and dissertation embargoes.* Retrieved from http://dissertationreviews.org/archives/11861

Turner, G. (2015). Learning to supervise: Four journeys. *Innovations in Education and Teaching International, 52,* 86–98. https://doi.org/10.1080/14703297.2014.981840

Turner, J.S., & Juntune, J. (2018). Perceptions of the home environments of graduate students raised in poverty. *Journal of Advanced Academics, 29*(2), 91–115. https://doi.org/10.1177/1932202X18758259

US Department of Health and Human Services, The Office of Research Integrity. (2015). *Case summaries.* Retrieved from http://ori.hhs.gov/case_summary

Uehara, E., Flynn, M., Fong, R., Brekke, J., Barth, R.P., Coulton, C., Davis, K., DiNitto, D., Hawkins, J., Lubben, J., Manderscheid, R., Padilla, Y., Sherraden, M., & Walters, K. (2013). Grand challenges for social work. *Journal of the Society for Social Work and Research, 4*(3), 165–70. https://doi.org/10.5243/jsswr.2013.11

UNESCO. (2007). *Global ethics observatory.* Retrieved from http://unesdoc.unesco.org/images/0015/001527/152796e.pdf

University of Washington Graduate School, The. (2015). *Financial support statistics.* Retrieved from http://grad.uw.edu/about-the-graduate-school/statistics-and-reports/financial-support-statistics/

University of Wisconsin. (2013). *The individual development plan.* Retrieved from https://d2olbli0yls2g4.cloudfront.net/wp-content/uploads/sites/329/2017/11/New_UW_IDPform-FINAL-fillable.pdf

Vaira, M. (2004). Globalization and higher education organizational change: A framework for analysis. *Higher Education, 48*(4), 483–510. https://doi.org/10.1023/B:HIGH.0000046711.31908.e5

van der Haert, M., Arias Ortiz, E., Emplit, P., Halloin, V., & Dehon, C. (2014). Are dropout and degree completion in doctoral study significantly dependent on type of financial support and field of research? *Studies in Higher Education, 39,* 1885–1909. https://doi.org/10.1080/03075079.2013.806458

van Hartesveldt, C., & Giordan, J. (2008). *Impact of transformative interdisciplinary research and graduate education on academic institutions* [Workshop report]. National Science Foundation.

Vassallo, P., Jeremiah, J., Forman, L., Dubois, L., Simmons, D.L., Chretien, K., Amin, A., Coleman, D., & Collichio, F. (2019). Parental leave in graduate medical education: Recommendations for reform. *American Journal of Medicine, 132*(3), 385–9. https://doi.org/10.1016/j.amjmed.2018.11.006

Walker, G.E., Golde, C.M., Jones, L., Bueschel, A.C., & Hutchings, P. (2008). *The formation of scholars: Rethinking doctoral education for the twenty-first century.* Jossey-Bass.

Wallgren, L., & Dahlgren, L.O. (2007). Industrial doctoral students as brokers between industry and academia: Factors affecting their trajectories, learning at the boundaries and identity development. *Industry and Higher Education, 21*(3), 195–210. https://doi.org/10.5367/000000007781236871

Walpole, M. (2008). Emerging from the pipeline: African American students, socioeconomic status, and college experiences and outcomes. *Research in Higher Education, 49*(3), 237–55. https://doi.org/10.1007/s11162-007-9079-y

Weaver, A.N., McCaw, T.R., Fifolt, M., Hites, L., & Lorenz, R.G. (2017). Impact of elective versus required medical school research experiences on career outcomes. *Journal of Investigative Medicine, 65*(5), 942–8. https://doi.org/10.1136/jim-2016-000352

Weidman, J.C., & Stein, E.L. (2003). Socialization of doctoral students to academic norms. *Research in Higher Education, 44*(6), 641–56. https://doi.org/10.1023/A:1026123508335

Weidman, J.C., Twale, D.J., & Stein, E.L. (2001). Socialization of graduate and professional students in higher education: A perilous passage? *ASHE-ERIC Higher Education Report, 28*(3). *Jossey-Bass Higher and Adult Education Series.* ERIC. Retrieved from https://eric.ed.gov/?q=).+Socialization+of+graduate+and+professional+students+in+higher+education%3a+A+perilous+passage%3f&id=ED457710

Weiler, W.C. (1994). Expectations, undergraduate debt and the decision to attend graduate school: A simultaneous model of student choice. *Economics of Education Review, 13*(1), 29–41. https://doi.org/10.1016/0272-7757(94)90021-3

Weisbuch, R., & Cassuto, L. (2016). *Reforming doctoral education, 1990 to 2015: Recent initiatives and future prospects.* Retrieved from https://mellon.org/media/filer_public/35/32/3532f16c-20c4-4213-805d-356f85251a98/report-on-doctoral-education-reform_june-2016.pdf

Wellington, J., & Sikes, P. (2006). "A doctorate in a tight compartment": Why do students choose a professional doctorate and what impact does it have on their personal and professional lives? *Studies in Higher Education, 31*, 723–34. https://doi.org/10.1080/03075070601004358

Wendler, C., Bridgeman, B., Cline, F., Millett, C., Rock, J., Bell, N., & McAllister, P. (2010). *The path forward: The future of graduate education in the United States.* Educational Testing Service.

Wendler, C., Cline, F., Kent, J., & Mageean, D. (2012). *Pathways through graduate school and into careers: Responses to the survey of graduate deans.* Educational Testing Service. Retrieved from http://pathwaysreport.org/rsc/pdf/survey_graduate_deans.pdf

Wheeler, E., & Arena, R. (2009). The impact of feeder school selectivity on predicting academic success in an allied health professional program. *Journal of Allied Health, 38*(3), 79E–83E.

Wiener, W.R., & Peterson, J.C. (2019). Strengthening the role of graduate program directors. *Innovative Higher Education, 44*(6), 437–51. https://doi.org/10.1007/s10755-019-09480-y

Wildgaard, L., & Wildgaard, K. (2018). Continued publications by health science PhDs, 5 years post PhD-defence. *Research Evaluation, 27*(4), 347–57. https://doi.org/10.1093/reseval/rvy027

Wilkins-Yel, K.G., Hyman, J., & Zounlome, N.O.O. (2019). Linking intersectional invisibility and hypervisibility to experiences of microaggressions among graduate women of color in STEM. *Journal of Vocational Behavior, 113*, 51–61. https://doi.org/10.1016/j.jvb.2018.10.018

Willetts, J., & Mitchell, C. (2016). Assessing transdisciplinary doctoral research. *Transdisciplinary Research and Practice for Sustainability Outcomes,* 122.

Willison, J., & O'Regan, K. (2019). *The researcher skill development framework.* Retrieved from https://www.adelaide.edu.au/melt/ua/media/765/rsd_4nov19.pdf

Wisker, G. (2015). Developing doctoral authors: Engaging with theoretical perspectives through the literature review. *Innovations in Education and Teaching International, 52,* 64–74. https://doi.org/10.1080/14703297.2014.981841

Wouterse, B., van der Wiel, K., & van der Steeg, M. (2017). Income differences between PhDs and masters: Evidence from The Netherlands. *Economist-Netherlands, 165*(4), 439–61. https://doi.org/10.1007/s10645-017-9304-9

Xu, D. (2017). Acculturational homophily. *Economics of Education Review, 59,* 29–42. https://doi.org/10.1016/j.econedurev.2017.06.001

Zhang, T. (2018). Graduate students identities in the intercultural practices on a US campus: A Q inquiry. *International Journal of Intercultural Relations, 64,* 77–89. https://doi.org/10.1016/j.ijintrel.2018.03.005

Zhou, E., Mitic, R.R., West, C.P.L., & Okahana, H. (2020). *International graduate applications and enrollment: Fall 2019.* Council of Graduate Schools. Retrieved from https://cgsnet.org/sites/default/files/civicrm/persist/contribute/files/CGS%20Fall%202019%20International%20Report.pdf?v=1

Zhou, E., & Okahana, H. (2019). The role of department supports on doctoral completion and time-to-degree. *Journal of College Student Retention: Research, Theory & Practice, 20*(4), 511–29. https://doi.org/10.1177/1521025116682036

Zimmermann, J., von Davier, A.A., Buhmann, J.M., & Heinimann, H.R. (2018). Validity of GRE General Test scores and TOEFL scores for graduate admission to a technical university in Western Europe. *European Journal of Engineering Education, 43*(1), 144–65. https://doi.org/10.1080/03043797.2017.1343277

Zou, C., Tsui, J., & Peterson, J.B. (2018). The publication trajectory of graduate students, post-doctoral fellows, and new professors in psychology. *Scientometrics, 117*(2), 1289–1310. https://doi.org/10.1007/s11192-017-2540-6

Index

www.ingramcontent.com/pod-product-compliance
Lightning Source LLC
LaVergne TN
LVHW090200080826
844660LV00013B/884/J

9781487508616